MONEY-GO-ROUND

Books by

JOHN J. FLOHERTY

Men Against Distance

Deep Down Under

Search and Rescue at Sea

Our F.B.I.: *An Inside Story*

High, Wide and Deep

Television Story

Aviation from the Ground Up

Watch Your Step!

Five Alarm: The Story of Fire Fighting

Get That Story: *Journalism—Its Lore and Thrills*

Shooting the News

Behind the Silver Shield

Flowing Gold: *The Romance of Oil*

White Terror

Men Against Crime

Money-Go-Round

Sons of the Hurricane

Decadrachma, 405–335 B.C.

MONEY-GO-ROUND

The Strange Story of Money

By

JOHN J. FLOHERTY

J. B. LIPPINCOTT COMPANY

PHILADELPHIA NEW YORK LONDON

PRINTED IN THE
UNITED STATES OF AMERICA

FOURTH IMPRESSION

Library of Congress Catalog Card Number 44-3757

To the Youth of America,
in whom I have an abiding faith.

IF THE AUTHOR MAY SPEAK:

Quite frankly, the subject of money had always seemed to me to be dry and without a spark of romance until a friend at dinner one evening pointed out that it has been the root from which has stemmed a large part of the romance and adventure in the literature of the ages.

In the lives of Midas, Croesus, and later Genghis Khan, money played a dramatic part. Thirty pieces of silver were Judas' undoing; pieces-of-eight lured the pirates of the Spanish Main into murder and marauding; Shylock's pound of flesh was collateral for borrowed ducats; the purchase from the Indians of the land on which New York City now stands was consummated for what would be about twenty-four dollars today. Novels and poems and plays without number have been written with money as the theme; hidden treasure, miser's hoard, wills and mortgages were but thematic variations.

Later it dawned on me that the curtain has been raised on the greatest drama in which the human race has ever participated—every living being, regardless of nationality, playing a part. Again money is the theme. The world is the debtor, bowed down by debts greater than the mind of man had ever dreamed.

In its search for peace and liberty, it has spent many times more than it owns. It is money well spent that none of us begrudges. It means, however, that for years to come we will feel the impact of war on our pocketbooks. Young and old, rich and poor, we will pay our share of the cost of victory. In doing so, we shall build a greater and a better world in which money will be, as it is today, a token of work done—that and nothing more.

I am indebted to Henry S. Morgenthau, Jr., former Secretary of the Treasury, for the assistance and material given me by various branches of the Treasury Department.

To Dan S. Eddins of Detroit, Michigan, I am also beholden for inspiration and material; and to the Chase National Bank my gratitude for the photographs of rare coins and early paper currency appearing in these pages.

J. J. F.

CONTENTS

Without money the pygmy tribes still travel long distances to barter the fruits of their labor.

1

A WORLD WITHOUT MONEY

PEARLY SHAFTS of light from an African dawn penetrated the tangled lace of the jungle and were caught on the ripples of a lazily moving stream. A canoe, gouged from a single log, slipped along noiselessly, driven by the deft paddle of a black man, Mbulo by name.

The rude craft was deeply loaded with edible roots, breadfruit, nuts and scarlet berries. A bundle of herbs bound with a strip of twisted bark surmounted the pile.

In the semidarkness ahead a violent swirl in the water caused Mbulo to lay down his paddle and reach for a long and slender spear that lay close at hand; then, poising to strike, he waited. An arm's length from the canoe, the gnarled head of a crocodile emerged suddenly from the water, its open jaws exposing windrows of savage teeth. The black man, throwing his full weight on the spear, drove it into the approaching reptile between and slightly above the eyes. In an instant the turbid stream was whipped into a lather of foam and blood as man and beast struggled for mastery. Lashing out with his ponderous tail, the infuriated crocodile struck the canoe, almost capsizing it. The black man held on to the spear a safe distance from the snapping jaws. He "played" the great beast as an angler plays a trout. After a final convulsive shudder the gray-white belly of the crocodile turned upward and its lifeless bulk sank slowly.

Then Mbulo continued his journey unperturbed, as if he considered the battle as just a part of his day's labor.

Several miles downstream where the river was wider and the jungle growth less dense, the right bank sloped gently to the water, making a fine landing place. A few strokes of the paddle sent the canoe bow first among the rushes that lined the shore and then on to solid ground.

Unloading the canoe, he carried its contents to a clearing a hundred yards from the water, making several trips along an animal run. Selecting a spot where the high grass had been trampled down, he arranged the roots and other edibles in piles, taking care to place the best in each pile near the top. Then he withdrew into the dense growth and waited, peering all the while around the edge of the clearing. Several hours passed. The sun, nearing the zenith, shortened the shadows to a fraction of their earlier length. A chattering monkey in the trees on the far side of the clearing brought Mbulo to the alert; his beady eyes swept the distant foliage and focused on a spot where he saw a vine move. Soon a bushy head was stealthily thrust forward. It was that of a tiny black man, a Tikki-Tikki. His face, ornamented with tribal scars, glistened in the tropical sunlight. After a careful survey of his surroundings, this newcomer tiptoed stealthily into the open and went to the spot where Mbulo's wares were on display. Carefully scrutinizing each pile, pinching the breadfruit and "hefting" the nuts, he went back to his cover. Presently he emerged, followed by two natives, one bearing the haunch of a large animal, the other a newly killed young antelope. These he laid beside Mbulo's store and retired with his men. As soon as they were safely hidden in the leafy cover, Mbulo came creeping from his hiding place and began an appraisal of the quantity and quality of the meat. After a moment's thought he took from each of his own food piles nearly half of what it contained and arranged a new group some distance away—then went back to

This strange coin, issued by the Romans, was known as "Oxen money." It was made of bronze and was nearly as large as a modern brick.

his hiding place. Almost immediately the little black stranger appeared again. He went to where the food lay, shaking his head and gesticulating wildly when he saw what Mbulo had removed from the original store. He took a quantity from each of the new piles Mbulo had set up and added it to the original from which it came. Mbulo grinned with satisfaction and came out into the open. He removed what remained of the second group of piles and loaded it into the canoe, then returned for the meat and placed that also in the dugout. The barter had been made without the exchange of a word.

This "dumb barter" has been practiced in many parts of the world since the earliest times. Herodotus, who lived more than two thousand years ago, told of "dumb barters" or "silent trades" he had witnessed in many lands.

While in the interior of Haiti not so long ago, I witnessed a barter scene not unlike that in which Mbulo bought meat with his vegetables. While I was photographing far up in the hills, a native woman, riding a donkey and leading a young goat, came along the trail and stopped at a palm-thatched hut. A native man appeared from the doorway and greeted her with a gruff *"bon jour."* Not another word was spoken. The man appraised the goat with the eye of a connoisseur, ran his hand over the animal's spine and flanks and then disappeared behind the hut. The woman, who had not dismounted, guided her donkey into the shade with her feet which were crossed over the animal's neck in the manner of the native riders. In a few minutes the man reappeared with four chickens, their feet trussed, their heads hanging downward. He laid them on the woman's lap. She ran her bony fingers over the breasts of the chickens and shrugged but did not utter a word. The man paused, eying her shrewdly and again disappeared behind the hut and returned a moment later with two young pullets. The woman made a grimace but did not speak. Again there was an awkward pause. The woman glanced disdainfully at the poultry and waved her hand impatiently as if to say, "Take them away." This time the man shrugged, elevating his shoulders and extending his palms as if he were saying, "What more do you want?" and moved as if to take back his fowls. The woman dug her heel in the donkey's neck and caused him to swerve; then with a leer of triumph threw to the ground the grass rope by which she had led the goat and rode away. *"Bon jour!"* she shouted as she departed.

Such transactions as these are not buying and selling in a true sense. They are rather an exchange of commodities consummated through a battle of wits. In barter the value of an article is not always determined in terms of intrinsic worth but on the need or desire for it by the purchaser and the labor involved in securing it by the seller.

I well remember an occasion in the north woods when, having lost our matches in a canoe accident, we exchanged a fine hunting knife and a box of cartridges for half a handful of wooden matches that cost but a few cents at the trading post. Three cold and miserable days had made warmth and hot food seem priceless. The trapper with whom we bargained saw nothing unfair in the transaction, as indeed there was not, since the value of an article is often enhanced immeasurably by location. A pannikin of water may

Egyptians weighing gold and silver. Weights were formed like animals.

well be worth many times its weight in diamonds in a waterless desert. A keg of nails purchased for a few dollars on the Eastern Seaboard often sold for as high as $400 during the gold rush days in California.

In primitive barter, the value of an article was largely determined by *need*. Mbulo, who had never heard of vitamins or proteins or calories, knew instinctively that he and his family needed meat to supplement their starchy vegetable diet. The pigmy, surfeited with the flesh of animals, felt the need of vegetables in his menu.

Besides the need-value, however, the barterer sets a labor-value on his wares, based on the effort and sometimes the danger of securing it. A succulent monkey, brought down by a dart from a blowpipe, was of less value in the pigmy's estimation than a luscious steak from the carcass of a young elephant. The monkey represented a pot shot in the jungle; the elephant, days of labor digging a pitfall and cutting with primitive tools logs and boughs with which to cover it.

Barter is sometimes frustrated when one of the parties has no need for the commodity offered by the other. This, however, does not prevent an eventual transaction. A few years ago a British military explorer in the heart of an African jungle found that in order to continue his journey up river he must have a large canoe. One of his bearers knew of a huge dugout that was owned by the headman of a village a day's trek from where the safari was camped.

On reaching the village, the explorer went to see the headman, a fierce looking savage surrounded by a chaos of wives, children, and war trophies. Seated on a log outside his palm-thatched hut, he eyed the Britisher suspiciously, glancing admiringly now and then at the fine pith helmet he wore.

After a peace offering of a few yards of colored cloth, a handful of beads and a cheap clasp-knife had been laid before him, he grunted with satisfaction. He leaned back against the hut and uttered a few guttural words which meant as plainly as if they had been in good English, "Well, what do you want?"

Through one of his bearers who acted as interpreter, the officer told the headman that he was in need of a large canoe to carry him and his party several hundred miles up the river.

The native ruler listened casually while he poured the beads from one palm to the other or tested the edge of the knife on the shaft of a long spear that stood beside him. He did not say a word, however. When asked if he had a canoe he would sell he merely grunted. It might have meant yes or no or perhaps.

The Englishman knew well the rules of the natives. "I will show you what I will give in exchange," he said through the interpreter. He gave a shrill whistle. From the jungle growth on the edge of the clearing came half a dozen of his black boys. They were loaded with narrow strap iron, coils of wire and cases containing gewgaws coveted by the average native. But the headman was not average. He eyed the barter goods with the air of a connoisseur and shook his head.

In the islands of the South Seas money is worn as ornaments by the natives. It is made of discs of pearl shell, dogs' teeth, boars' tusks and shells of many varieties.

"More?" inquired the interpreter.

Again the chief shook his head, this time decisively and uttered the one English word he knew. "Ivory!" he shouted, "Ivory!" and retired into his hut.

The Englishman, having no ivory, realized that it would be futile to try to bargain with the headman or to attempt to make him change his mind. He motioned to his bearers to gather up the trade goods and, with complete nonchalance, led the way back into the jungle. The first step of the barter procedure had been completed.

Next day the exploration party arrived at another and smaller village. There the officer found a man who had ivory—a goodly store of it—but he would accept only red cloth for it, three bolts to the tusk. The explorer had only a few bolts of blue cloth and there was no use in wasting time in offering the trade goods of which he had plenty. He learned, however, that there was another village down river that was inhabited by members of a savage tribe whose treachery was well known throughout the district. Unconcerned by the prospect of trouble, he led his safari in the direction of this new village. All went well until the procession was within a mile or so of the cluster of miserable huts. The officer and his gun-bearer strode along a hundred yards ahead of the heavily loaded black boys. As they reached a small clearing which was no more than a widening of the animal trail they had followed, an arrow shot past the Englishman's head and buried itself in a near-by tree. Without so much as a pause in his stride, he drew the shaft from the tree trunk, broke it in two and flung it disdainfully aside. Looking neither to the right nor to the left, he swung along as if nothing unusual had happened. As they approached the village they could see the women and children scurrying to cover. Word of the party's approach had evidently preceded it.

The explorer went directly to the hut of the chief. It was larger than the others and stood near the center of the circular village. There was not a native in sight. He entered the low doorway, followed by the interpreter.

In one corner the chief sat, or rather squatted, on a low stool, the legs of which were rudely carved to resemble those of an animal. In the opposite corner were piled many bolts of cloth, most of it red. With the aid of the interpreter the palaver began and came to the point at once. Would the chief trade some of his cloth for much iron and wire, enough to encircle the village? The headman's eyes glittered greedily as he thought of the spearheads, arrowheads, knives and other implements he could make and trade for other commodities more valuable than his cloth. "How much?" he asked shrewdly.

The Britisher replied, "As much as one of my black boys can carry for a day." This was usually about sixty to seventy pounds.

Meantime the bearers with the iron and wire came as prearranged and threw their loads on the ground outside the hut with great clatter. The chief rose slowly and eyed the metal, appraising it in terms of cloth, then appraising the cloth in terms of skins he had traded for it. He brought forth a dozen bolts and laid them on the ground beside the iron—and waited.

"Not enough!" said the Britisher sharply. Four more bolts were added and again the chief waited.

"Not enough!" repeated the officer. The chief shrugged as if to say he would give no more. With a show of impatience the explorer ordered his men to pick up their loads and take them away. The chief hurried into the hut and reappeared with two more bolts, setting them on top of the others.

"Done!" said the officer. "It's a trade." Not until the safari was well in the jungle did he smile with satisfaction at having out-traded the chief.

Next morning the exploration party arrived at the village where ivory could be secured for cloth, and again there was a battle of bluff that ended with complete success for the Britisher. With the ivory now in his possession he felt sure that the canoe would soon be his and that they could start up the river the next evening.

As the explorer and his train of bearers came to the outskirts of the village, they were surprised to see the huge canoe propped up outside the chief's hut. From its still wet surface they could see that it had been taken from the water when their approach was announced—a precaution most likely against possible theft.

As the bearers carrying the ivory lined up in front of the chief, he carefully scrutinized each tusk and seemed satisfied with its quality and quantity, then he turned his attention to the explorer, eying greedily the white pith topee on his head.

Clay tablets of which the original of this photograph is one, were used extensively as money by the Babylonians.

"Here is your ivory. We will take the canoe." The Englishman's words were translated by the interpreter. There was silence for a moment, then the chief shook his head decisively. The explorer, although alarmed, remained calm—even nonchalant. It seemed as if the exhausting labor of securing the ivory had gone for nothing. Turning to the interpreter he snapped, "What more does he want?" The native, wise in the ways of the African, whispered, "Topee! Him want topee."

Calling a black boy who had a kit bag balanced on his head, the explorer told him to lay it on the ground and from it took a battered felt hat. Approaching the chief, he removed his topee and placed it on the chief's head. The chief grinned with satisfaction as he watched the officer put on his old felt hat; his native acquisitiveness and vanity had both been satisfied. At a signal, a hundred natives swarmed around the canoe and bore it to the river. The complex barter had been finished.

The origin of barter is hidden in the mists of the far past. The neanderthal man, whom we will call Neander, undoubtedly said to his wife at the approach of winter, "The cold weather will soon be here, my dear, and our furs are about worn out. I will take a slab of our mammoth meat up into the hills and trade it for wolf pelts." While returning with the pelts he came upon a neighboring cliff-dweller who had acquired considerable skill in making stone hatchets. In fact the hatchet-maker was then putting the finishing touches on a murderous weapon. It was just what Neander needed in his perpetual hunt for meat. Those that he had made were clumsy and ineffectual; besides, fashioning them consumed much time that could be devoted more profitably to hunting.

"I will give you pelts for your hatchet, neighbor," he said in grunting monosyllables.

The hatchet-maker paused while this strange offer penetrated his undeveloped mind, then he replied frankly, "Why should I, who am not as strong as you, risk my life battling with wild beasts? I will make your weapons and you, Neander, will do the hunting. Then I will share your meat and your skins and, perhaps, a part of your cave." That in all likelihood is how the first barter was made—barter in which each man contributed the fruit of his labor to the welfare of both.

While man had only primitive wants—food, clothing, shelter—the barter system was adequate. As his gregarious instinct asserted itself, however, and he began to live in groups which grew from two or three closely related families into villages and towns, he found that the mere exchange of commodity for commodity did not always work out to the benefit of the community. The basket-maker who needed bread for his family, took his wares to the only baker in the village who at that moment needed several baskets which he took in exchange for a number of loaves of bread. Although the transaction was equitable, the basket-maker found himself, a week later, without bread, while the baker had baskets that would last several years. In the case of the butcher, the baker and the candle-stick-maker, the butcher and baker could get along very well since they could exchange commodities every day, while the candlestick-maker would have a hard time getting meat and bread because his wares lasted a lifetime. This baffling situation led eventually to the establishment of trading fairs to which the people flocked with all kinds of commodities. There they could spend days inspecting and bartering amid the endless variety of wares that had been brought to one place from hundreds of miles around.

During the Middle Ages these barter fairs grew to huge proportions. The Hanseatic League, a powerful organization of traders, established great warehouses all over northern Europe. These were really indoor fairs at which great quantities of goods of all kinds were displayed for barter. The use of money, of which there was very little, was forbidden. All accounts were settled entirely on a barter basis.

These early gatherings were rollicking affairs. There were feasting and dancing and matrimonial match-making. Mountebanks, jugglers and itinerant musicians entertained the crowds for profit. A singer of ballads in which love and valor triumphed was rewarded with bread or fruit or a handful of corn. A favorite entertainer was the contortionist who placed a goblet of strong drink on the ground behind him, then bending himself backward until his lips reached the goblet, emptied it without touching it with his hands. The performer supplied the goblet, his audience refilled it and the performances for the day ended when the "artist" had drunk one too many.

The state, county, and church fairs of today stem from these barter fairs of the Middle Ages where business and pleasure were combined. While the barter motif has almost entirely disappeared from the modern fair, it has manifested itself in virulent form in another phase of our community life. The first Christmas gifts of oil, frankincense, and myrrh were borne by the three Wise Men to the manger at Bethlehem as a token of veneration and allegiance to the Christ Child whom they acknowledged as the new-born King. During the centuries that have passed since the birth of the infant Jesus, Christianity has perpetuated the adoration of the Magi by giving gifts at Christmastide as a gesture of peace and good will. Of late this kindly custom has degenerated into plain barter in which gift is matched with gift and value with value with little trace of the beautiful symbolism that marked the custom for centuries.

So deep is the imprint of this world-old barter on our modern social life, it manifests itself often where least expected. The gracious Mrs. Brown gives an intimate little dinner party to which she invites her friends, the Greens, the Blacks and the Whites--all charming people. She insists on the finest cuts from her butcher and the most succulent vegetables from her green grocer and sets her kitchen at high tension during the preparation of the meal. Her best china, silver, glass and napery are brought out for the occasion. The table is set with infinite care, and the flower arrangement is perfect to a petal. When the guests arrive, they find Mrs. Brown in her most attractive dinner dress, a charming hostess whose genuine hospitality is well known to them. The dinner goes off without a hitch; the food is excellent, the table talk sprightly and interesting. It is, in fact, a great success. After bridge and a little music the guests depart, delighted and refreshed by a most entertaining evening.

Then the barter begins. Within a few weeks Mrs. Green gives a dinner party to which the Browns are invited. The food, the table appointments and the general air of hospitality equal those of Mrs. Brown. This is followed by a dinner given by Mrs. Black and, of course, Mrs. Brown is among the guests. Weeks later Mrs. White remarks to her husband, "We *owe* the Browns a dinner. Suppose we ask them over Wednesday evening." And so, on Wednesday evening the cycle of barter is completed.

The good Mrs. Brown would be shocked if it were suggested that she had bartered a dinner and had received three in return.

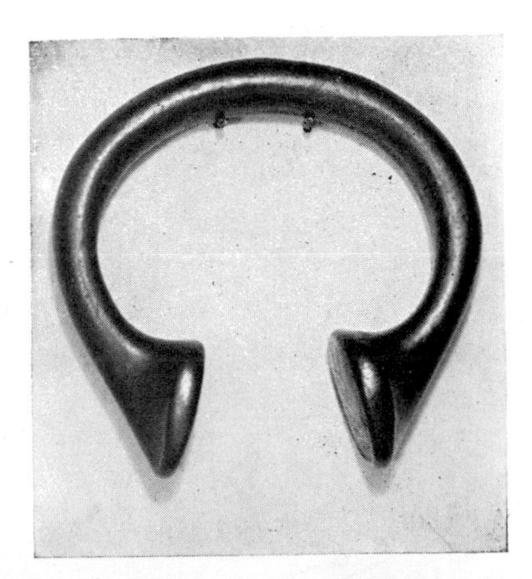

Ring money, often used as an ornament on nose or ears by natives of the Ivory Coast, Africa.

No.
£255.

STATE of M

IN Behalf of the State of Massachusetts-Bay, I the Subscriber do hereby p
to pay unto Thomas Hoover or to his Or
on or before the First Day of March
with Interest at Six per Cent. per Annum: Both Principal and Interest to be p
Five Bushels of CORN, Sixty-eight Pounds and four seventh Parts of a Pound o
shall then cost, more or less than One Hundred and Thirty Pounds current Mo
Times and an Half what the same Quantities of the same Articles would c
One Thousand Seven Hundred and Seventy-seven, intitled, "An Act to prever
Value of every Pound of the Sum herein promised, to be determined agreeable t
ment of the Balances that may appear to be due by Virtue of a Resolution of the
Seventy-nine, to this State's Quota of the CONTINENTAL ARMY, agree
with a Sum of Money for that Purpose."

Th. Dawes
R. Cranch } Committee

A fine example of Colonial paper money—a two-hundred-fifty pound note, issued by the state of Massachusetts in 1780. Actual size.

Of course, no such thought ever entered her mind nor did it occur to the others. They are all victims of the relentless social edict; an invitation to a good dinner calls for one in return.

One of the most insidious forms of barter in modern times is trading-in a used car when a new one is purchased, or swapping one used car for another. These transactions usually demand that the purchaser also pay a sum of money to boot, precisely as little Willie

[...]CHUSETTS BAY

The FIRST Day of JANUARY, A. D. 1780.

[...]blige Myself and Successors in the Office of TREASURER of said STATE,
[...]m of Two hundred Fifty five
[...] of our Lord One Thousand Seven Hundred and Eighty three
[...]hen current Money of said STATE, in a greater or less SUM, according as
[...]en Pounds of SHEEPS WOOL, and Sixteen Pounds of SOLE LEATHER
[...] then current Prices of said ARTICLES—This SUM being THIRTY TWO
[...]ices affixed to them in a Law of this STATE made in the Year of our Lord
[...] and Oppression" The current Prices of said Articles, and the consequent
[...]f this STATE, intitled, "AN ACT to provide for the Security and Pay-
[...]ASSEMBLY of the Sixth of February One Thousand Seven Hundred and
[...]Recommendation of CONGRESS, and for Supplying the TREASURY

Witness my Hand
H. Gardner Treasurer

swaps his sling-shot for a baseball bat, giving a dozen marbles to boot—that is, to equalize the exchange.

So extensive is this automobile barter, there are several billion dollars continually tied up in the second-hand car market.

Our word "barter" comes from the Italian *"barattare"* which Florio defined in his dictionary (1598) as meaning "to barter, truck, chop and change one thing for another." Others of its ancestors,

No (419) 20s

THIS Indented Bill of Twenty Shillings due from the Massachusets Colony to the Possessor shall be in value equal to money & shall be accordingly accepted by the Treasurer and Receivers subordinate to him in all Publick paym:ts and for any Stock at any time in the Treasury. Boston in New-England February the third 1690 By Order of the General Court

Elisha Hutchinson
John Walley
Tim Thornton
} Comittee

This photograph was made from an actual specimen of colonial and continental paper money issued in 1690.

however, do not seem to be without tarnish since they connote trickery, sharp practice, cheating. One of these forebears is the old French word *"barater"* meaning to cheat; another the Greek word πϱαττεἰν (*prattein*) meaning to use sharp practices or tricks; and the Gaelic word *"brath"* means just out-and-out treachery.

Perhaps that is why professional barterers have always been looked upon with suspicion. Their creed has always been, "Get the best of the bargain!" Haggling, squabbling and sometimes murder were everyday occurrences among them in early times. Each belittled the goods of the other, and charges of trickery, cheating and lying flew thick and fast. A running fire of abusive and variegated language was kept up during transactions. The loudest mouth or the vilest tongue attracted the largest audience and was invariably applauded by the crowd that gathered to "see the fun" and to bedevil the victim into a poor bargain.

There is a fish market in London called Billingsgate. Built on the bank of the Thames close to London bridge, it was opened in 1558 as a landing stage for provisions. More than a hundred years later it was converted into a free and open fish market where fishing smacks deposited each day's catch. When the owner of the smack had unloaded her on the dock, his wife, known as a "fishwife," took charge of the load and carried on the rough-and-tumble task of selling it. A throng of fishmongers and housewives milled around among the piles of fish over which the fishwives presided. The air was saturated with smells and noises. Everybody shouted at the top of his voice. Above the hubbub the harsh cackle of the fishwives cursed and cajoled. These amazons were noted for their profanity and abusive vocabulary; they tongue-lashed competitors and customers alike. Those who looked as though they had money to spend they beguiled with sugary flattery, while those who had goods to barter were treated as public enemies to be berated and belittled while greedy eyes appraised the goods they had brought for barter. Frequently a fight occurred between fishwife and customer, and soon became a free-for-all. When order was restored, the customer's barter property had usually disappeared, but not a tail nor a fin of the fishwife's stock had been touched. "Billingsgate" soon became synonymous with abusive language and may be found in the dictionaries to this day.

The first coins were issued by the Lydians in 700 B.C. They were made of electron, a natural alloy of gold and silver.

2

MONEY MAKES ITS BOW

As EARLY civilization developed in different parts of the world and the needs of the people became more complex, it was evident that the barter system was inadequate since it provided no equitable means of establishing value. The lonely ermine hunter, after months of hardships in Arctic wastes, received a few trade commodities, mostly food, for his pack of skins. Months later, these skins enriched a royal robe and were considered worth their weight in gold. These inequalities were accepted as a matter of course, since barter was the only means of exchange.

Then one day an unknown man, probably a Chinaman whom we will call Choo Ling, became the world's first economist. As he looked around at his friends and neighbors, he observed that they all worked for the things they possessed. Some tilled the soil, others built houses, or boats, or one-wheel push-carts; still others made beautiful things in metal or wood or stone. The things they harvested, or made, or created constituted their wealth. Why then should not this wealth be reckoned in terms of labor? The more he thought of it, the more he became convinced that labor performed should be the common denominator that would govern the value of commodities and remove from the exchange of goods the hit-or-miss methods that had been practiced for many centuries.

Having arrived at that premise, he spent weeks pondering over a method of putting his theory into practice. A man of great wisdom, he visited his neighbors and talked with them at length about his proposed plan. Some nodded assent, some were alarmed, and a few did not understand what he was talking about. In each house, however, he saw skins piled up—in some instances to the rafters. They were the skins of animals that had been bought by barter, butchered and eaten long since. They had barter value no longer, since every family in the village had more skins than it could use. There were goatskins and sheepskins, kidskins and lambskins, thousands of them. In the house of Ching Foo, he picked up a fine goatskin and said, "You received this goat in barter for cloth"—for Foo was a weaver— "Your customer used all the cloth you gave him, yet you used only part of the goat he gave you. The cloth cost you many hours of labor; therefore, this skin represents a part of that labor. It is not valueless; it is a token for, say, a yard of cloth."

Ching Foo, who was prominent in village affairs, saw the point and soon spread the word through the community that the skins piled in every house were tokens of labor performed—they were, in fact, money. And so they were, and continued to be, money for many centuries thereafter. For it must be remembered that money, which must not be confused with coins, is a token of work done, whether it be in the form of skins or oxen, dogs' teeth, iron rings or cash.

More centuries passed. Man learned that he could plant the seeds and edible roots of many things that grew wild, and for which he had to roam far to gather enough for a single meal. This was one of his great discoveries. A small bag of grain which he spent many days collecting, when scattered on the fertile ground outside his hut, provided him in a few months with a goodly store of food. A single grain of wheat yielded an ear on which were forty or fifty grains. The addition of his labor to the bag of wheat increased his wealth in grain forty or fifty times.

Slowly, but surely, he learned how to till fields and grow crops.

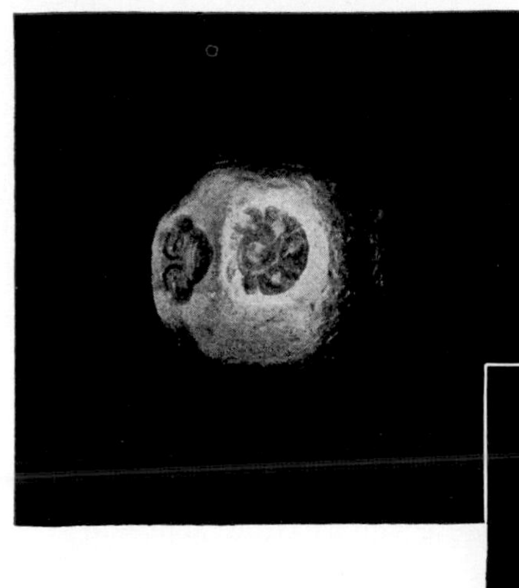

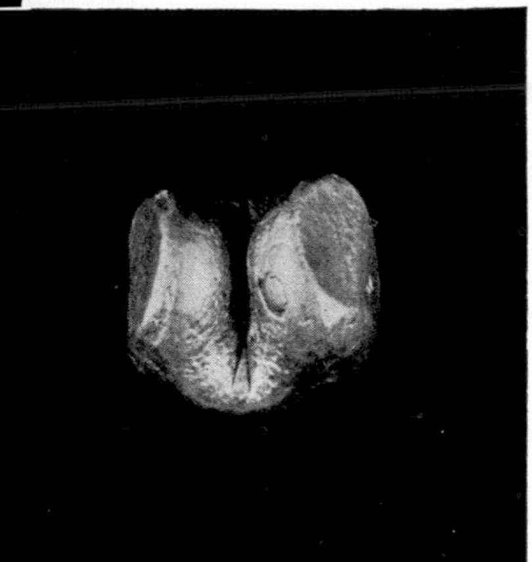

This "bullet" money from Siam was often used in gambling in much the same way as dice are used. To prevent gambling, it was pinched so that it would not roll.

This left him little time for hunting wild animals for food. He abandoned the spear and the bow for the spade, and gradually entered a pastoral state; he became a farmer. He abandoned his hut in the forest or his cave at the foot of a cliff. He came into the open and there built himself a house and a place to store the crops he had grown. He took himself a wife and raised a family, half a dozen sturdy boys and girls; for these had increased his wealth by the labor they contributed. Alone he could till ten acres; with the help of his family he could till thirty. Now, however, instead of one, he had eight mouths to feed and eight bodies to clothe. He also had to provide shelter and sleeping accommodations for his brood. This was no longer a serious problem, however, now that the family labor had brought him wealth.

From time to time he sold a part of his stored grain wealth for money tokens; in his day, skins. When a hunter came by with a fat young doe on his shoulder, he bought it with so many skins. When he needed cloth for clothing, he and one of his sons threw two bundles of skins on their backs and set out for the village where lived the weaver. When his granary needed a new roof, he called in the builder who lived down the valley and set him to work. The builder went into the near-by woods and hewed the trees, adzed them into rafters, or whipsawed them into boards, and built them into a new roof, using wooden pins instead of nails. When the job was finished, the builder was paid off in skins. Thus, these men shared the farmer's wealth, receiving skin money in return for their labor.

The names of all the men in these transactions are well-known family names today. They are Farmer, Hunter, Weaver, Carpenter or Sawyer. Others who contributed their skill to the community welfare are Butcher, Porter, Mason, Smith, Baker, Taylor, Miller, Shoemaker, Barber, Wheelwright, Wagoner and many others. Men who practiced trades or arts were known by the name of their pursuit.

Here and there throughout the world, as the result of over-supply, the money value of skins declined. It was also discovered that it was possible to have wealth increase itself under certain circumstances solely through the passage of time. This was the first inkling of *Interest.* Cattle and sheep were used instead of skins in many places and with many advantages. In the first place, this four-legged money was easy to transport when one went to market and, secondly, it bore interest in the form of new-born animals that increased in value as they grew older.

In time, the practice of using livestock for money spread through the Eastern Hemisphere. The western half of the world had not yet been discovered.

During this period when cattle were used as currency, many words came into being that are in use today. For instance, the word "chattel" meaning personal property, comes directly from the word "cattle." In Latin, the word for money is *"pecunia"* which in turn comes from the word *"pecus,"* meaning a herd of sheep or cattle. When sheep or cattle were stolen, the theft was referred to as *"peculatum"* from which comes our word "peculate" meaning the theft of money. In those early days, as now, livestock was counted by the head. They spoke of a hundred head of cattle. The Latin word for head is *"caput"* and cattle were *"capitale,"* whence comes our modern word, "capital." So it becomes evident that in ancient days, cattle and money were synonymous. So closely were they associated that the Greeks and Romans stamped their coins with the image of an ox.

In those very early days, practically all commodity moneys had a food or clothing value. During hard times the oxen could be eaten and the goatskins could be converted into serviceable jerkins or breeches. In this, the early currencies, the four-footed wealth, had a decided advantage over the metallic money of the later centuries, since in times of stress or famine a man could eat his fortune or with it protect his body from the winter blasts. This he could not do with silver or copper or precious gold. In those primitive days starvation was always lurking just around the corner. When it struck as it often did, the only man who was really wealthy was the man with enough food to tide him over the crisis.

Almost as important as animals was grain currency. In fact, in some districts and at certain seasons it was preferred because it was more convenient in making small purchases than were animals. The purchase of a cart or a suit of armor was easily negotiated since the cart or the armor was worth so many oxen or sheep. When, however, a hat or a knife or a drinking vessel or any article of less value than oxen or sheep was purchased, the parties to the transaction had to revert to barter. With wheat or corn, purchases to any amount, great or small, could be made in a satisfactory manner.

Corn, or maize as it was called, was a highly negotiable form of currency. It was extensively used by the ancient Greeks, and was later adopted by several northern and central European countries. Even as late as the middle of the last century, Norwegian banks accepted deposits of corn which could be borrowed, or loaned, or used in transactions just like any other form of money.

Throughout Central America and Mexico, and even in some parts of North America, corn was used as money for many years. In 1641 the Commonwealth of Massachusetts found itself literally without coins. The small stores of metal money they had brought over from the mother country dwindled rapidly in the purchase of goods from Britain, while Britain forbade the export of coins to the Colonies. In desperation, the Colonists passed laws making corn legal tender.

Thus, the acceptance of corn in the payment of all debts became obligatory. Nearly a hundred years later the people of Maryland, finding themselves in the same predicament, passed similar laws.

It is startling to find that three of the most advanced of the earliest civilizations—Rome, Greece and Egypt—used human beings as money. In those days a man's wealth was often appraised by the number and the physical condition of his slaves. Slaves were not only an index of a man's wealth, but were used as a medium of exchange in the larger transactions. This slave money had the advantage of fractional values. A healthy muscular young male was accepted as the equivalent of two of lesser strength and endurance. He was also considered equal in value to two women or two women and a boy, depending on what man-slaves were bringing in the open market. It was not unusual for a slave-owner to purchase from a cattle-raiser so many head of oxen at a price of so many slaves and then send the slaves for the cattle, after which they returned to their new master only to be sold for cloth or grain. The Greeks, who specialized in a high physical standard in their slaves, supplemented them with copper vessels as a fractional currency. A Grecian nabob, purchasing a gold embroidered garment of fine cloth, may have paid for it with a Herculean slave and a number of copper pots. If it were of extraordinarily fine workmanship, he probably threw in an ox and a pair of unshorn sheep for good measure.

The Romans also used "living money," as cattle and sheep were called. In the fifth century B.C. they paid taxes, fines, and other moneys due the State in cattle. Many centuries later this same method of paying taxes was used also, as in the early days of Massachusetts.

Both the Romans and the New Englanders gave up the practice for the same reason: Then, as now, the tax collector was considered fair prey for those who strove to pay as little in taxes as possible, while remaining within the letter of the law. The tax laws called only for the payment of taxes *in cattle*. They did not stipulate age or weight or physical condition. The tax dodgers—and they were many—saved their old and undernourished animals for the tax collector, so that the State was often in possession of great herds of scrawny cattle of little more value than their tallow and hides.

As population grew, and buying and selling became more com-

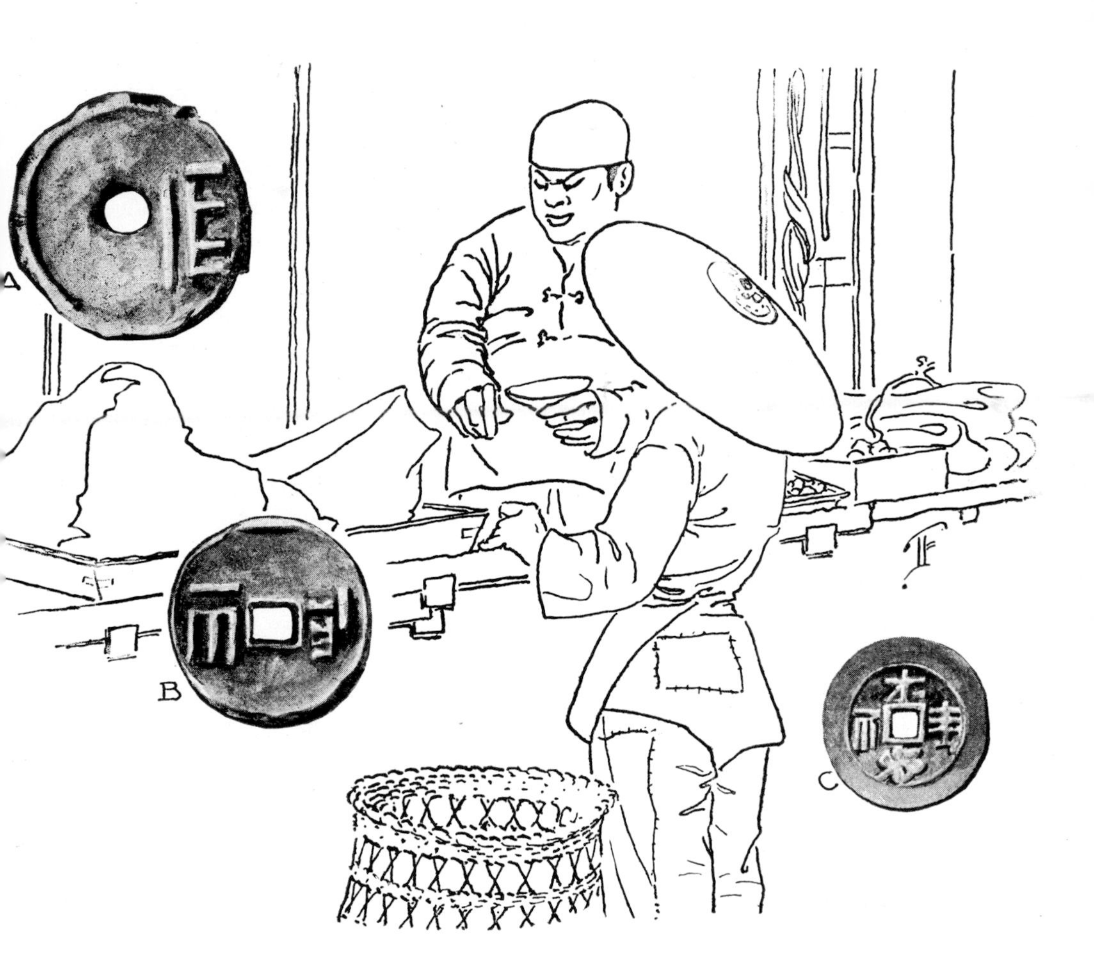

Chinese "cash:"

A. Round hole money—480 B.C.

B. Square hole money—160 B.C.

C. Square hole "cash"—1875.

plex, the problem of a convenient money became acute, particularly in urban communities.

It was all very well for the farmer to draw on his cattle capital and drive a few head to town when he wanted to purchase supplies for his farm and family. The town dweller, whose house was huddled against his neighbors' and who owned no grazing land, was at a disadvantage. He was an artisan, a merchant, or a laborer whose commodities or work had no fixed value. He sold the fruit of his effort for whatever he could get, whenever or wherever he caught a customer, for truly, in those times trade was altogether a catch-as-catch-can affair. Trading was often done in the wine shops, purchaser and seller hoping that the other would become befuddled first and so become easier prey. Again the Chinese—or was it the Lydians, no one knows—conceived the idea that animals or growing things were, at best, cumbersome and often impractical tokens of man's labor: cattle needed feeding and constant watching, while grain was perishable and required extensive storage space properly weather-proofed.

Even in those primitive days, men and women went in for personal ornamentation. First worn as charms or amulets, the ornaments were brightly colored buds or blossoms which wilted in a few hours. In time, flowers gave way to more durable talismans. Pebbles and pellets of colored clay were strung on animal tendons and worn as necklaces not unlike some of the costume jewelry we see worn today. This primitive ornamentation was not prompted entirely through vanity. A certain pebble, valueless in itself, when credited with bringing good luck to the hunter, was valued beyond price. A rounded piece of crystal, when worn by a sick person who recovered his health, was believed to be a mighty barrier against disease and was cherished as a priceless possession through life. This belief in the supernatural has survived through the ages, and still exists even among otherwise intelligent people. When watch chains and watch fobs were the style only a generation ago, a watch *charm* was considered quite the smart thing to wear. A banker whom I knew, a highly intelligent man, once showed me a battered and worn coin, to the possession of which he attributed much of his success. When he was a young man, he told me, he lost his job through the failure of the concern for which he worked. After weeks of heart-breaking effort, he found a job in a

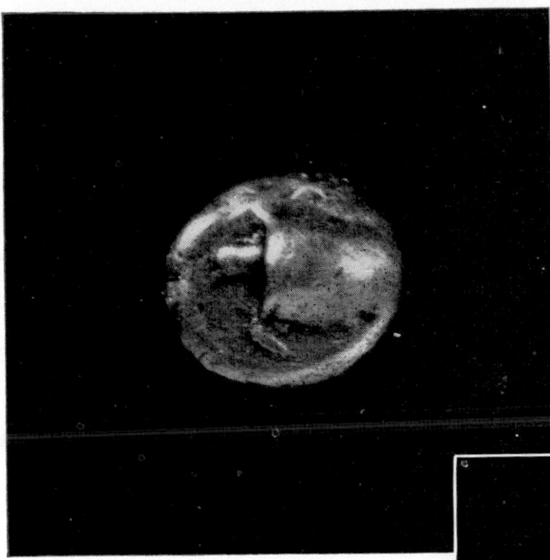

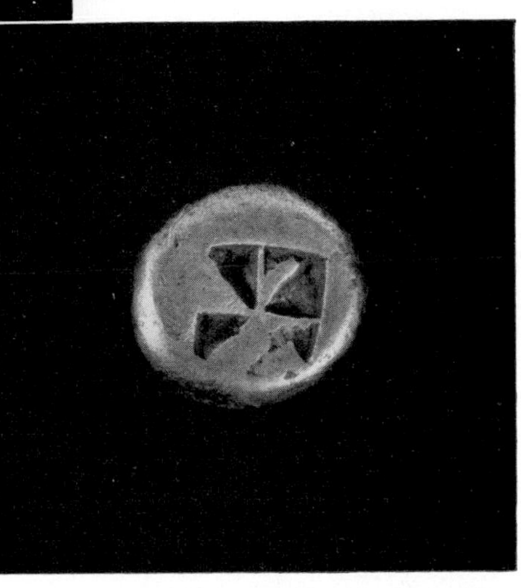

Photograph shows a drachma, coined 200 B.C. This is the earliest silver coin.

lumber yard. Before he had received his first week's salary, he arrived one morning to find the place a mass of smoldering wood upon which firemen were still pouring water. Again weeks passed while he walked the streets searching for employment. He brooded over the streak of bad luck that frustrated all his effort. Then, one morning as he was starting out on his daily rounds, he saw a coin lying in the gutter. It was a battered and badly worn half-dollar. On examining it he found that the date on the coin was 1870, the year of his birth. He thought hopefully that this might be an omen, a turn in his luck, and so it proved to be. His first call that morning was at a small bank where, to his delight, he was employed as porter, messenger, and general handy man. Things went well with him, so well in fact, that in less than three years he was assistant cashier. He guarded his good luck piece as if it had been a fortune, but one day it disappeared. At first he was panicky then he reconciled himself to its loss. After all, it was just another coin, he told himself.

One morning before opening time, the president informed him that the bank had consolidated with a larger and more influential bank that had been a strong competitor for years. And then, breaking the news as gently as possible, the banker told him that his services would not be required in the new set-up.

When the shock of the bad news had passed, he remembered the loss of his lucky piece and soon became obsessed with the idea that it was responsible for his predicament. Times were bad; jobs were few; the outlook was dark indeed.

A few mornings later—it was to be his last day at the bank—the porter came to his desk and laid the lucky piece before him. "They tell me this belongs to you," he said and left. The assistant cashier was so overcome, he barely thanked the porter. His spirits rose, his courage returned; he had no fear of the future. That evening he entered the president's office to say goodbye. "Hold on a moment," said the banker, "there have been a few changes in plans since I spoke to you. Since you are familiar with many of our accounts, we have decided to keep you on. You will report at the other bank on Monday morning." Again, according to my friend the banker, the lucky piece had saved the day. During the many years that have ensued, this hard-headed businessman has retained his faith in the potency of his lucky coin which he still carries in a corner of his wallet.

Countless people still believe in the power of certain minerals, whether they be in the form of jewels or coins, to influence their lives for good or evil. The famous Hope diamond is an example of this primitive hocus pocus. There is a legend that the former owners of the bauble met misfortune or came to an untimely end. Its present owner, however, undisturbed by its gruesome history, wears it on the slightest provocation without any tragic result.

I have digressed merely to show that the early peoples who adopted metal money were not very different from many of us today who convert large amounts of wealth into ornamental gewgaws or at-

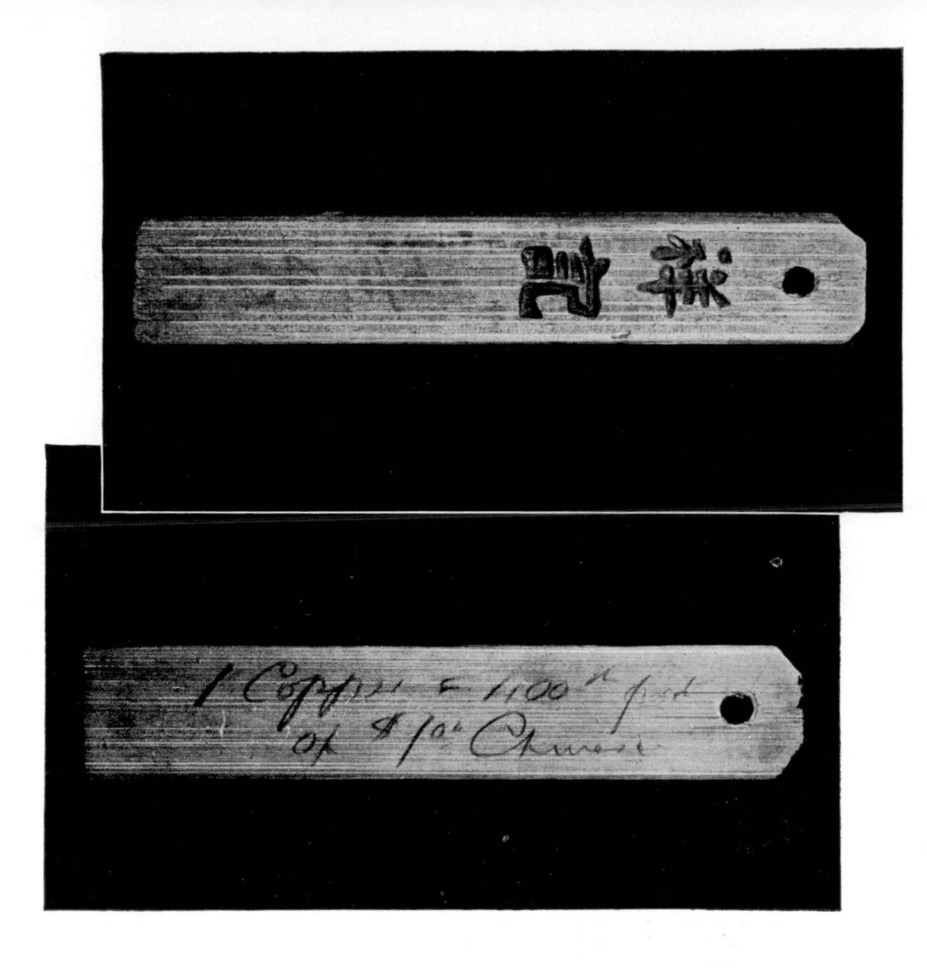

Bamboo money as used in China. Its denomination is "one copper."

tribute supernatural powers to it. There are those who will not accept a two-dollar bill because they consider it unlucky. Others will not accept a knife or sharp instrument as a gift unless they give the donor a coin which is supposed to prevent the cutting of friendship. In many stores and offices the first dollar taken in when they began business is framed and preserved as a kind of talisman that will bring good luck to the enterprise.

Not more than twenty years ago, during a slump in business and industry, a New York jewelry manufacturer came into possession of an ancient Chinese ring on which were engraved Chinese characters. The ring was beautiful in design and proportion and showed the skilled hand of a fine craftsman who had long since gone to his fathers. An admirer of fine craftsmanship, the manufacturer became curious about the origin of the ring and the meaning of the inscription. He went to see a Chinaman who was then a student at Columbia University. The Chinese, a scholarly person well versed in the lore and traditions of his native land, on looking at the ring, smiled wistfully and paused as if forgotten memories had been stirred. "You have here a good luck ring," he said, examining the gold circlet with a touch of homesickness. "Rings of that design have been made for hundreds of years in China."

"Did they bring good luck?" asked the jeweler jokingly. The Chinaman's face became serious. "Who knows?" he said as he handed back the ring.

On returning to his establishment the jeweler ordered a replica of the ring put in production at once. He also ordered his advertising department to publicize it in a whimsical vein as the "Chinese good luck ring."

In due time the ring was ready for the sales department, and the advertising was begun. Orders began to come in immediately, at first by hundreds and then by thousands. Soon the factory was swamped with orders that came pouring in daily. The brisk business continued for months.

The jeweler, his sales staff, and advertising staff were astonished at the returns. An honorable man, he feared he had been unwittingly guilty of deception. He ordered the words "good luck" dropped. Then came the real surprise. Letters began to arrive, thanking him for the good luck the ring had brought the wearers. Hundreds of them came; they were almost hysterical over the change in fortune. Some sent their blessings; others their undying gratitude. But the jeweler knew that their good fortune lay not in the ring but in an improvement in the country's business and thousands of new jobs.

In Sir George Macdonald's book, *Evolution of Coinage,* he suggests that a coinage was instituted in China as far back as 1091 B.C., but the earliest coins of which we have specimens were minted in Asia Minor about 700 B.C. by the Lydians or Ionian Greeks. The button-like coin is made of electron, a natural alloy of gold and silver which was found in the streams and mountains. At that period it is evident that both gold and silver were reasonably plentiful, since they were used for ornaments and vessels; copper, too, was in common use. It was for that reason probably that the alloy electron was used—it was scarcer and consequently more valuable.

In the fourth century B.C., India developed a system of coinage that differed from all others then in existence. The "coins" were square or oblong bars of metal. On each bar was stamped by royal decree its weight and value, as a guarantee to the person to whom it was payable.

We are completely in the dark as to when gold, silver, and copper were first extracted from the earth or melted and refined for use in making ornaments and such utility articles as cups and armor. What we have gathered from ancient writings indicates that long before history began, they were coveted for their beauty and for the many properties that made them ideal mediums for display of the craftsman's skill. Artist vied with artist in designing rings, bracelets, ceremonial cups and household vessels. Then craftsman vied with craftsman in rendering the designs in the precious metals.

The art manifested in these objects was not entirely art for art's sake. A certain quantity of the raw metals in the form of ingots or rude coins was worth so much; fabricated into articles of ravishing beauty, it was worth so much more. Art in those days had an intrinsic value when expressed in gold or silver and brought a handsome return for those who invested in it. Each article was molded and finished to a certain weight, the value of which was fixed. It could be thrown back into the crucible and taken out again as a formless lump of metal, but its fixed value remained the same. The addition of art to the metal created an increment, a sometimes immeasurable increase in value. This early form of investment was practiced extensively. Many converted a large part of their wealth into gold, and then had it fashioned into articles both useful and ornamental. In this way, they could get use and pleasure from their capital, assured that in an emergency they could convert it into bulk metal with an established value.

Small articles like rings, bracelets and brooches, made in certain weights, had standard value and were frequently used as money. In *Genesis* we find that the servant of Abraham presented Rebekah, the

Salt, a valuable commodity down through the ages, is used as money in Sierra Leone, West Africa. Packed in bamboo cylinders about a yard in length, it is used as we use dollar bills.

bride of Isaac, with an earring of gold weighing half a shekel and two gold bracelets weighing ten shekels. In this case shekels were really weights that eventually became coins with a value equivalent to $10.88 in American money. The word "shekel" is still used extensively as slang for money.

Among the early businessmen of the Middle East, scales and weights were as necessary in their financial transactions as are the cash register and adding machine of today. Again we find in *Genesis* that when Abraham purchased a field from Ephron, "Abraham weighed to Ephron the silver which he had named in the audience of the sons of Heth, four hundred shekels of silver, current money with the merchant."

The use of weights and scales for gold and silver brought the invention of coinage as we know it today appreciably nearer, yet strangely, the Egyptians, the Babylonians and the Assyrians, who introduced the system of weights to their money transactions, did not progress beyond that point. The idea of placing an official or government stamp on the metal, and so converting it from a weight into a coin which was also a weight, must be credited to the Lydians. Herodotus, who knew his world better than most men of his day, assures us that these Lydians were the first to mint and use a coinage of gold and silver. He also informs us that they were the first retail merchants.

The metal used for their first coins was electron, known today as white gold, a natural alloy containing about 73% of gold and 27% of silver. At that time gold in Asia Minor had about thirteen times the value of silver.

Those electron coins caused widespread confusion. Buyers and sellers, accustomed to transacting business on a gold or silver basis, had to pause while they figured out the worth in gold or silver of the electron coins involved in a purchase or sale. Few were expert in arithmetic. Those who were, profited; those who were not, lost. The coins, however, were circulated by royal edict and there was not much the people could do about it.

A century and a half later, Croesus, king of Lydia, whom we still mention as a symbol of fabulous riches, called in his chancellor and a few gray-bearded advisers to discuss the monetary affairs of his kingdom. An able ruler, he was well aware of the dissatisfaction of his subjects with the electron currency and of its retarding effect on domestic business and trade with neighboring countries. Coming to the point at once, he ordered all electron coins recalled to be redeemed in gold or silver of which the royal treasury had a great store.

On hearing the edict, the chancellor bristled. Had the king gone mad? Such extravagance would bankrupt the country, and besides he was doing very well for himself exchanging gold and silver for electron coins at rates far below their face value. "Your Majesty!" he growled.

But the king would permit no interruption. He ordered that coins of gold and silver be struck, each stamped with the royal mark to guarantee its weight and, consequently, its value. When the new coins were issued, there was great rejoicing among the people. Each man knew his wealth; he had the king's word for it. He could buy and sell, and lend and borrow, and know at the end of the day where he stood financially. The new coin, called a *croeseid,* was not much to look at. It was in the form of a rough oval, no two of them exactly alike, but all of them containing the same amount of gold or silver to the weight of a spider web.

So popular did the coins become, they were accepted and welcomed in neighboring countries. The island of Aegina off the coast of Greece issued a silver *stater* and stamped it with a sea turtle, the symbol of the god of weights and measures. Some historians suspect that Croesus may have borrowed his idea of issuing standardized coins from Aegina. This is unlikely, however, since Croesus was by all odds the smartest man of his day where money was concerned.

The method of making these coins was slow and cumbersome. After the precious metal had been weighed carefully, it was roughly molded into crude blanks, usually in the form of disks. A metal die, presumably iron, on which the design of one side of the coin was engraved in intaglio, was placed on an anvil and a gold or silver disk was then placed on the die. Then a punch, on the end of which was engraved the other side of the coin-to-be, was fitted on the disk and held in place by hand. When all was in readiness, another coiner, usually of powerful build, swung a sledge-hammer and struck the punch a mighty blow. From this primitive coinage operation we still preserve the verb "to strike" when we speak of making coins or medals.

About the time standardized coins were being introduced, Greece was approaching the peak of her power. Art flourished, beauty became a commodity whether expressed in marble or metal; wealth was everywhere.

Jealous of the success their little neighbor Aegina was having with her silver stater, the mighty Greeks followed suit but on a gigantic scale. Besides the coinage issued by the State, a flood of metal money flowed from cities, towns, colonies, and even from individuals. More than 120,000 different kinds of coins were issued in varying quantities.

This jamboree of coin making, while economically confusing, had its better side. The coiners developed great skill and artistry. They abandoned the punch and die method because of the crudeness of

A decadrachma from ancient Syracuse. It is of the period 405-335 B.C., but is still considered one of the finest examples of the coiners' art. Reverse of coin shown on title page.

the finished coins. Instead, they used two dies placed face to face with the metal blank between them. The dies were struck a powerful blow with a heavy hammer. The result was a coin on which the design was centered. In many of the older coins made by the punch method, a part of the design was lost through the careless or inept placing of the punch.

The most widely used coin among the Greeks was the *drachma.* Prior to its use, in fact, before the introduction of coins of any kind, the money in everyday use was nothing more than short lengths of iron or copper wire not unlike our tenpenny nails. These were known as *oboloi* and were measured out by the handful in payment for purchases. A handful of *oboloi* became a standard unit of money and was called a *drachma,* which meant literally "a handful." When the new coin was minted, it was given the value of a handful of the old iron money. It was also given a weight value that was based on the Babylonian *mina,* sixty of which were equivalent to our pound. The silver *drachma* was, in weight, one-hundredth of a *mina* and would be worth today about eighteen or twenty cents in our money.

So pronounced was the impact of early Greek civilization on the countries of the world, many of them, centuries later, adopted this twenty-cent value for their basic coins. The krone of Austria, the franc of France, the lira of Italy, and the coins of several other countries are valued during times of normal exchange rates at about twenty cents. In fact, it is said that our own American dollar is simply five of these *drachmas.*

The best known of the early Athenian coins was the *tetradrachm,* equal to four *drachmas,* often mentioned as the Athenian dollar. It carried on its obverse side a delicately executed head of Athena, the goddess of wisdom, and on its reverse was the image of an owl, emblem of the city of Athens. The sheer beauty of the coin made it a general favorite, not only throughout the Grecian colonies but throughout the world, although at that time, five hundred years before Christ, the world was a small place. The silver of the *tetradrachm* was the purest and its weight was accurate to a hair.

The *tetradrachm,* however, was for the well-to-do and was of little use to the majority of the people. In those days a man who earned a *drachma* a day was considered fortunate indeed. To meet the needs of the less opulent, a silver coin, the *obol,* with a value of about three cents, was produced. Now three cents worth of pure silver, even in early Greece, did not give the coiner much to work with. The best he could do was to produce a little silver wafer no larger than the end of a lead pencil and no thicker than a rose petal. Small as they were, the man-in-the-street welcomed these poor man's coins. He had grown tired of carrying around the iron and copper nails, the *oboloi,* he had been using as money. Besides the *obols* were the modern idea; in the fifthy century B.C. Athens was truly modern.

No sooner were the coins in circulation than complaints began to pour in. The coins were so small and so light that the owners lost them continually from purse and pouch and pocket. Put to it for a safe place to carry small change, many of the Athenians carried the tiny coins in their mouths; it was not uncommon to see a purchaser drop the *obols* from his lips into the palm of the person from whom he had purchased an *amphora* of oil.

There was a lively rivalry between the cities of Athens and Corinth. In commerce, industry, art, and athletics the struggle for supremacy was continuous and at times belligerent. It was inevitable, therefore, that the cities would vie in the quality and beauty of their coins. While Athens had a head start in the art of mintage, it did not take the Corinthians long to catch up and at times outstrip their rival. About 550 B.C. Corinth issued a silver stater that for sheer beauty of design has seldom been equaled even by the mints of today. As each new coin came into circulation, groups assembled in the streets, the marketplace and at the game arenas and hotly discussed the merits of the new piece of money and compared them with the latest coin issued in the rival city. It is thought that this rivalry was responsible for the large output of new issues.

During that period Grecian coins bore the images of mythological characters or animals symbolizing them. Occasionally, by way of a change, an ear of wheat, a dolphin, a horse, a ship or some equally extraneous subject was used in commemoration of a particular event. Not until Alexander the Great came on the scene, about 336 B.C., did the face of a living person adorn a coin. Alexander, like some of his later prototypes, had a good sense of publicity. In fact, he may well be called the patron saint of press agents. A strong candidate for popularity, and with unlimited power, he conceived the idea of putting his portrait in the pockets of his people. Choosing a *tetradrachm* as the ideal publicity medium, he instructed his mint master to prepare a sketch for the proposed coin, the obverse bearing Alexander's portrait, the reverse a portrait of Zeus, supreme god of the Greeks. The artist who executed the sketch, more familiar with Zeus than with his king, depicted the god as the incarnation of power befitting a deity, while his rendering of Alexander showed a mere man, mortal and finite.

Calling his mint master and the artist to his chamber, the king chided them on the poor job they had done in presenting him as the running mate of the great Zeus; the comparison would make him a laughing stock. As he fumed he grasped a lion skin from his couch and flung it over his head and across his shoulders. "See!" he shouted. "Draw me as Hercules, mighty and unconquerable. My people want their ruler vigorous and indomitable!"

And so Alexander the Great, stamped in enduring silver, went out into the homes of his constituents, where the *tetradrachms* he adorned meant security. What a modern candidate for office would give for such publicity!

While the economy of early Greece was closely allied with the arts, it is not recorded that the artists whose work spread the fame of the country to the ends of the earth, profited materially. Praxiteles, who breathed life into cold marble, and whose statues are regarded today as beyond price, was glad to receive a commission to make the model for a coin since he was paid for it. The Acropolis and the Parthenon are today monuments to the forgetfulness and thanklessness of a people. The thirty classic figures in stone buried by the Athenians after the battle of Salamis, and found in 1888, were carved from unyielding stone by sculptors whose names were never known, not even in Athens. The craftsmen who hewed boulders into beauty as expressed in capitals, pillars and pediments of the Parthenon were

A silver thaler issued during the reign of Maria Theresa, 1717-1780. A fine example of the coinage of that period.

forgotten men even in their day. It is doubtful if the best of our moderns could hold a candle to them. These ancients worked for the glory of work and gave their souls and their bodies to the creation of beauty that would live, as live it did. They devoted their days to glorifying their Greece, and at night, to keep body and soul together, they toiled by the light of a flickering lamp, creating coins and vessels and the many things of beauty that are cherished in our museums today. I know several contemporary artists whose earnings for a single month represent more hard cash than was probably received in a lifetime by the artists who created many of the treasures of Greece that will live forever.

Perhaps it was this neglect toward those who had helped make their country the pivot of civilization that proved to be the weak spot in the armor of the Greeks when the Roman legions began their campaign of conquest.

In the sixth century B.C., while Greece was enjoying at least the rudiments of an advanced civilization, the Romans were still quite primitive. Commerce was carried on largely on a barter basis, and such money as they used was in the form of slaves, oxen, sheep and goats. Keeping an eye on her Grecian neighbors across the Ionian Sea, she noted the growth of their commerce, the extension of their colonies and the improved economic status of the people and credited the advancement to the extensive coinage system that had been established. Determined not to be outdone by her rival, Rome decided to issue coins of her own. Entirely unversed in the art of coinage, her initial attempt resulted in crudely cast pieces of bronze without beauty or much intrinsic value. They were coins, however, certified by the State to have a monetary value, and were used in the general course of trade for nearly two hundred years.

About the middle of the fourth century B.C., piqued by the beauty and the general acceptance of Grecian currency, the Romans went into coinage in a big way. Determined to outdo their rivals at all costs, they minted a bronze coin—the *aes*. It was a huge affair weighing a pound (Roman) and in spite of its cumbersome bulk, it was a coin in every sense of the word. Made of bronze, it took a powerful man to carry enough of them to buy a toga, or a cask of wine, of which the Romans in those days were fond. The *aes* was minted under contract to the State by mint masters who had an eye for profit. Each issue was made a little lighter than the preceding one, but the nominal value remained the same. So gradual was the debasement of the coin, few noticed it and no one—not even the State—seemed to object, since in its lighter form it was more convenient to carry, and saved bronze for use in breastplates, helmets, sword hilts and shields. Little by little, the lightening process continued until 89 B.C. when the once gigantic *aes* weighed only half an ounce. It is generally conceded that the pound weight of this unwieldy coin was the inspiration for the name of the British pound.

Still determined to have a comprehensive coinage, the Romans soon supplemented the *aes* with issues of smaller fractional coins of one-half, one-third, one-sixth and one-twelfth of its value, none of them comparable in design or workmanship to the coins of Greece. The *aes* and its related coins, however, seem to have been adequate, since no other coin of note was minted for nearly two centuries. In 268 B.C. the Roman army, having grown to huge proportions in numbers and power, had become a heavy drain on the monetary resources of the State. Even in those days when the country was burdened with a horde of spendthrifts in high places, the lowly soldier was deemed worthy of his hire. To pay off the army, a new coin, the *nomos,* was minted. It was so successful as currency that another coin, not unlike it in weight and value, was struck soon after. The new coin became the most widely circulated of all Roman coins. Known as the *denarius,* it had a face value of about eighteen cents. Just as our popular name for a five-cent piece is a "nickel," so the *denarius* became known to the populace as a "penny." Years later when the British coined a penny, it was called a *denarius.* The British symbols to this day for pounds, shillings, and pence are £. s. d., the initials of Libra, shillings, and *denarii.*

Eventually the *denarius* became the foundation on which the Roman coinage was built. It was minted in scores of designs, each a memorial to some outstanding historical event. The assassination of Julius Caesar was the inspiration for one of these coins. It showed on one side the head of the mighty Caesar, and on the other the daggers that did the dirty work. A little later, when the Roman Senators had officially deified the great Caesar, a comet appeared in the sky one evening and held the attention of the awe-struck populace for seven nights. This was too good an opportunity for the

An example of royal cheating. This Spanish dollar was issued in 1780 during the reign of King Charles III. The coins sent to the Spanish possessions in the West Indies had a large piece of silver cut from the center. This coin became known as the Guadeloupe "Holey Dollar."

coiners to miss; a commemorative *denarius* was designed at once. When the coin appeared, it showed a head of Caesar on one side and a blazing comet with seven rays on the other.

During the pre-Christian era, Rome made much of its pagan gods. Not satisfied with temples, and festivals, and amulets by the hundreds, they honored their numerous deities on their coins, thus fulfilling a twofold purpose—paying religious tribute to their gods and building up a store of good luck for those fortunate enough to possess the coins. This practice of reverence on coins continues to this day. On British coins may be found the letters F.D. (Fidei Defensor)

Defender of the Faith, a title bestowed on Henry VIII, and carried on British coins ever since. We still carry on our American coins testimony of our faith in the Deity by the simple sentence, "In God we trust."

The many wars in which the Romans were engaged over a long period brought with them the same financial stringencies that confront the warring countries of these times. The same inequalities in the pay of those engaged in the conflict also existed. In Caesar's day, the makers of the weapons of war profited handsomely, as they do today, while the wielders of them were given a pittance in payment for their prowess and their lives. So niggardly was the pay of the Roman legionnaire, he was reimbursed for his services to the State, not in coins which were reserved for the non-combatants, but in salt of low grade. This payment in salt was known as *salarium*, from which comes our word "salary." The wounded and weaklings of the soldiery were said to be "not worth their salt," a common expression of disgruntled employers in this, the twentieth century.

The Greeks, and later the Romans, seem to have been adept in the art of propaganda; their name and fame were on every man's tongue even in the farthest places, not for their culture so much as for their skill in war and their ruthlessness in battle. The Romans held the world in a hypnosis of fear. This domination influenced the politics, the economics, the laws and the coinage of the weaker nations. Even when conquered, as they were eventually, they left their mark for centuries on the coins of the world. Some of the modern American and British coins still carry Latin inscriptions.

Russia and Scandinavia stood firmly opposed to the so-called classic influence in their coinage, even refusing to employ the widely used gold, silver, and bronze of other countries, or to follow the circular form. They chose iron as their coinage metal and minted it in elongated hexagons, something like an ace of diamonds with the upper and lower ends of the pip cut off. They called it a *ruble* or *rubli* which means "a piece cut off." Russia, like other countries, used skins as money for many centuries. As a matter of convenience and preservation they developed a tanning process, whereby the skins were converted into leather. At first whole hides were used, but peasant and prince found them awkward to carry. They had advantages, however. They could be cut into small pieces for

The Romans commemorated their prowess on the sea by striking an "aes" which bore the two-faced god Janus on one side and a galley—an oar-propelled ship—on the other.

change or they could be converted into shoes or harness or military accouterments. Eventually the government gave this leather money its official approval by stamping each piece. Thus, one of the wiser government heads reasoned that since it was the government stamp that gave each piece of leather official value, the size of the piece was not important; so the sides of leather were cut into small pieces about the size of a special delivery postage stamp and duly impressed with the government's seal. In this way leather money was converted into leather coins that supplemented the metal rubles until as recently as 1721. The modern Soviet ruble is a fine-looking silver coin, about the size and, normally, the value of our half-dollar.

Leather was also used in France during the reign of Louis IX, otherwise known as St. Louis of France (1225-1270). The sainted king found himself, as did many other monarchs, short of cash with which to pay his army. At that time silver was the most desirable currency metal. Then, as now, the cost of wars was high. Silver coins became more and more scarce; so scarce, in fact, that the royal treasury found itself unable to meet the army payroll. Small as the soldier's pay was—a few cents a day—it was an obligation that had to be met. A disgruntled soldiery was worse than useless; it was dangerous. The king rummaged around for all the silver he could lay his hands on. Vessels, ornaments, sword hilts, buckles and a heterogeneous mass of odds and ends made of silver were melted down. The resultant amount of minted coins was still far short of what was required to pay the army. The king, in spite of his saintliness, was blessed with a worldly shrewdness. Discovering that a silver coin, the *gros tournois,* which was about the size of our quarter, could be drawn into a fairly stiff wire nearly two feet long, he hit on the idea of converting his store of silver into miles of silver wire. This he had cut into lengths of about three inches, on one end of which was made a small loop. To the loop was fastened a leather tab, stamped with the State seal and given the royal blessing. These leather-tagged slivers of silver were the moneys with which the troops were paid. They were tokens of the soldier's labor in the service to his country.

Russia and France were not the only countries that, on occasion, turned from metal to less durable material in their coins. About the middle of the sixteenth century, the Dutch city of Leyden was

Pirate silver, pieces of eight, was welcomed by the Colonies.

hemmed in on all sides by the Spaniards. During the siege, the city was reduced to starvation. Many who had the foresight to lay in large stocks of food and other necessary commodities made huge profits by selling for hard cash at fabulous prices. Since the city was cut off from outside communication, the war profiteers were soon in possession of most of the city's cash. There was no metal available that could be used for coins to replenish the supply. The city's chief industry was cloth weaving, for which it was famous throughout Europe. The owners of the weaving establishments paid their workers in cloth, they, in turn, bartered it for bread. Since several bolts of cloth were demanded for a single loaf, many went hungry.

When things looked blackest, a scholarly looking young man, carrying a book under his arm, came before the city council. When asked to state his case, he laid the book on the table and opened it. The stolid burghers were startled when they saw that every eight leaves of the book had been pasted together and pressed into a kind of cardboard. "Here is something that will take the place of metal," he said. "Books are plentiful in Leyden. Make your coins from this compressed paper, stamping it as if it were metal."

"But why use books?" asked a graybeard. "Why not plain paper?"

"Because," replied the young man, "our books are among our most valuable possessions, some of them are more valuable than their weight in metal. And besides," he continued triumphantly, "the printing between the pasted pages will baffle counterfeiters."

Then and there it was decided to collect all the books in Leyden and convert them into coins, just as if they had been so much metal.

The story of the book-paper coins of Leyden would not be complete without mentioning that, when the siege of the city was raised, the inhabitants were rewarded for their courage and resourcefulness. A university, now the most important in Holland, was founded in 1570 and a library created that boasts today of some 200,000 volumes.

No less unique than the paper coins of Leyden were the bronze coins of Sweden about the middle of the seventeenth century. At that time the country was ruled by a woman, Queen Christina, who combined her queenly virtues with business acumen. When she took up the royal scepter, one of her first endeavors was a survey of the coinage system. She found the country flooded with a hodge podge of copper coins with little value. So great was the number of the coins necessary to carry on the financial affairs of the country, the mints worked day and night to supply the ever-increasing demand.

She also found that one of the most valuable properties held by the crown was a large copper mine at Falun. So unstable was the copper market that the royal mine, notwithstanding its great output, often found itself showing a loss. The great cost of minting the copper coins also caused a considerable loss.

Putting two and two together, the Queen saw that if the royal treasury was to be strengthened, mints and mines must work together. How to accomplish this, however, was a problem that caused the Queen and her counselors sleepless nights. All were convinced that whatever was to be done must be drastic and unprecedented. Government officials then, as now, leaned toward the conservative; traditions must be preserved at all costs. The Queen, unfettered by those inhibitions, struck out along lines that were not only drastic but startling.

One morning her breakfast was brought to her bedside. The food was laid out daintily on a silver tray, in the center of which was engraved the royal coat-of-arms. As her eye caught the heraldic device, the morning drowsiness left her; she suddenly became filled with energy. "Take this tray away," she said sharply, "and bring it back empty!" The maid-in-waiting did the Queen's bidding, won-

Tally sticks such as these were used as a form of money by the Bank of England until the middle of the last century.

dering if her sovereign had suddenly gone mad. When the empty tray was returned, the Queen sat gazing at it, deep in thought. Finally she arose, a look of determination on her face. "Send the chamberlain at once," she said to her lady-in-waiting. "Yes, Your Majesty," replied the startled woman. The appearance of the chamberlain in the Queen's apartment at such an early hour was quite unheard-of.

The chamberlain, a weazened little man with snow-white beard, entered the room all a-quiver. Such peremptory orders from his Queen foreboded something beyond his comprehension.

"Have the council assembled immediately. There is urgent business!"

"But—Your Majesty!" the little man trembled visibly.

"You will do as I say, dear Olaf," said the Queen with the purr of a tigress.

In quick time the members of the council were assembled in the Queen's anteroom. Each looked inquiringly at the other as if to ask, "What's in the wind?" and received in return a blank stare. When ushered into the presence of her majesty they could scarcely bow, so great was their astonishment. The Queen stood at the head of a long table with a large breakfast tray in her hands. She came to the point at once. "Gentlemen," she began, "I have called you here to announce that I have at last determined on the coin about which we have been thinking for so long." Smiles of approval went around the table. "It will be in the value of eight *dalers* and will be minted in bronze."

"In bronze, Your Majesty!" the counselors chorused. Then one of them addressed the Queen. "That would be impossible, Your Majesty. Eight *dalers* in bronze would be as much as Your Majesty could lift!" Ignoring the interruption, she continued, "It will be in size the dimensions of this tea-tray. The royal insignia will be stamped on each corner and in the center the weight and value. The copper used in the bronze will come only from the government's mine and the price of copper will be stabilized thenceforth. That will be all, gentlemen!"

When the men of state had left the royal presence, they shook their heads in bewilderment. "Eight *dalers* in bronze!" exclaimed one of them, "Why, it will weigh forty-five pounds!" And so it did. And besides it measured thirty inches by sixteen inches.

Stone money from the Island of Yap. The large "coin" weighs 120 lbs., the smaller 14 lbs. Compare size with cocoanut on right. Some weighed several tons.

When the gigantic "plate" coins were issued, the people gasped. For a time they could not make up their minds whether the plate money was a practical joke, or practical economics with which the country had had but little experience. Soon, however, as reports of the huge coins spread through the kingdom and into the neighboring countries, the eight-*daler* plate was eagerly accepted and continued as sound money for more than a century.

During the thousands of years that men have used money in one form or another, its most necessary attribute has been value. As a general rule the value of a piece of money, whether it were an ox, a pelt, a string of shells, or a twenty-dollar gold piece, was determined by the amount of labor it represented.

The labor involved in raising, feeding, and herding a number of oxen was, let us say, a hundred times greater than in hunting a

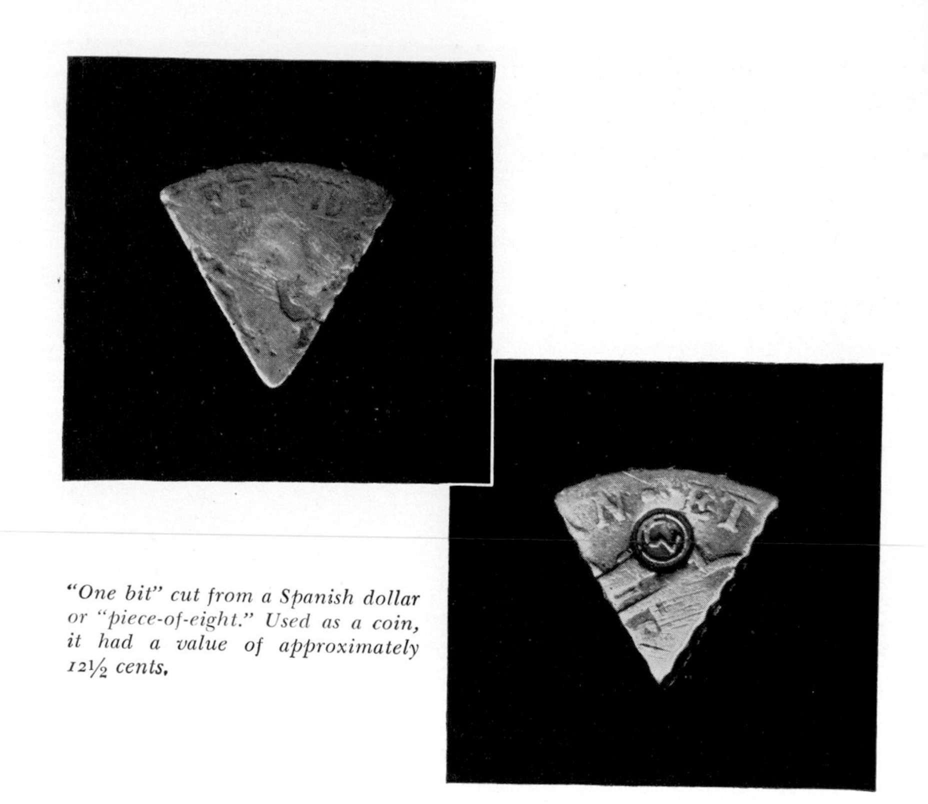

"One bit" cut from a Spanish dollar or "piece-of-eight." Used as a coin, it had a value of approximately 12½ cents.

similar number of beavers for their skins. An ox, therefore, should be worth a hundred beaver skins. On the other hand, a prime pelt of an Arctic fox often called for a hundred times more labor to secure than the catching of a beaver. Therefore, it was only fair that the same ox that was worth a hundred beaver skins could be purchased with the pelt of a single fox. In like manner, silver and gold were more valuable than copper and iron, because, like the Arctic fox, they were rarer and, consequently, took more labor to secure.

In the Australasian archipelago there is an island called Yap where large stones are used for money. The stone "coins" are of calcite and range from six inches to twelve feet in diameter. In form they are an irregular oval with a large hole in the center. The larger coins are considered preferable to the smaller ones since they cannot be stolen easily. Originally, the inhabitants of Yap made hazardous three-hundred-mile canoe voyages over the open sea to secure the stones from which to make their money. Later on, an Irish trader brought great slabs of calcite to the island and traded them for cocoanuts. There was no calcite to be found on Yap. The natives chiseled the huge stones into coins of various sizes and values.

In this far-away island wealth is created only through labor. The collective wealth of the natives represents the total number of hours spent in making it. While more complex, our monetary system differs but little from that of the Pacific island. The composite wealth of our country represents the sweat and labor that its people have expended during hundreds of years in building our industries and commerce, and in developing our arts and sciences.

The celebrated pine tree shilling coined in New England in defiance of a monarch.

3

Money of one kind or another had been in use in the Old World two thousand years before Columbus set out on his great adventure. The European countries had well-established currencies, some better than others, but all of them reasonably adequate for domestic trade and in some cases international commerce.

The financial affairs of a country in those days did not differ materially from those of today. Extravagant governments, wars, crop failures brought on inflations and consequent depressions. It was during one of these periods of money stringencies that Columbus petitioned Queen Isabella to back his expedition to the East Indies by way of a short cut to the west which he believed existed. The Queen, like most people in her day, had no knowledge of geography and no interest in the scientific aspects of the explorer's project. She merely saw an opportunity to enrich the royal treasury, then at low ebb, through the comparatively small investment of less than $7,000.

Columbus himself was paid 1,500 *pesetas* or about $300 a year as

EVERY MAN HIS OWN MINT

commander of the *Santa Maria.* The captains of the other ships, *Nina* and *Pinta,* received $150 a year each, while the crew members were paid about two dollars and fifty cents a month and were given food to the value of one dollar and fifty cents for each man. The cannons on all three ships cost 14,000 *pesetas,* less than it costs to fire a single shot from one of our modern naval guns.

Columbus, following the custom of the period, carried a supply of trade goods, vividly colored cloth, scraps of shiny metal, bushels of glass beads and a quantity of eye-catching odds and ends, surefire barter bait for the natives. It was with this collection of "five-and-dime" commodities that Columbus traded for food for his return voyage and for evidences of wealth in the newly discovered land to lay before his royal patroness who, as he well knew, had a sharp eye for business.

Rumors of Columbus' discovery of a new continent passed quickly from mouth to mouth and from country to country, for it is recorded that within a decade or so fishermen from Spain, Portugal, Ireland and the Scandinavian countries headed their shallops into the west in quest of fish, the predominant food of most European countries. In 1577 a fleet of nearly four hundred vessels was engaged in fishing off the coasts of what are now New England and Nova Scotia. In wintertime they hurried their catches back to the home ports, depending on the frigid weather of the North Atlantic to keep them fresh. During the warmer months they unloaded their boats on the bleak shores and set up their fençelike "flakes" on which they hung the fish to cure in the sun.

When the storms came many vessels of the fleet were wrecked on the rocky shores. The few of their crews that escaped death adapted themselves to the bleak country, made friends with the Indians, bartering with them for food and furs the few possessions they had salvaged. They were simple fishermen, however, unversed in trade. Thankful to be alive, they had no profit motive in their dealings. Food was plentiful; venison, wild fowl and salmon were to be had in abundance. Inured to the hard life of the seafarer, they enjoyed the comparative comfort in which they lived in the new land. The bountiful harvest of fish along the shores of Newfoundland attracted fishermen from all the maritime countries of Europe. Those that returned were loaded to the decks with haddock, halibut, and codfish.

Beaver skins, millions of them, were used as money in northern United States and Canada from early days to the middle of the nineteenth century.

Even in those days English vessels were noted for their stanchness, and English navigators for their daring. Soon the British flag flew from the mastheads or gaffs of many of the craft in the great fishing fleet. So glowing were the accounts of the new country brought home by the returning fishermen that the British government dispatched Sir Humphrey Gilbert to take possession of Newfoundland and establish an English colony there.

Trade followed the flag. Sir Humphrey, a forceful man, soon established a profitable barter business, not only with the natives but with the fishermen colonists. Hard and unyielding, he made life miserable for those who would not see his way. In fact, many of the colonists deserted him and in the face of great hardships and many dangers set out for the less rigorous country at the mouth of the Kennebec River. Here they established a community known as Popham, where they were soon joined by the crews of two vessels sent over by the Plymouth Company to found a fishing colony on the coast of Maine.

The colonists accepted their hard lot with fortitude and by dint of sweat and sacrifice, made themselves reasonably secure from want in a few years. One fact, however, caused them much concern. Being without a vessel seaworthy enough to cross the ocean, they were cut off from the motherland. Undaunted they set to building a stanch vessel that would give them escape should it become necessary and also enable them to sail to the fishing banks and do some trading along the coast. In the fall of 1607 the ship was launched and christened *Virginia*.

Almost simultaneously with the launching of the *Virginia*, a settlement was made at Jamestown, Virginia. The settlers were an oddly assorted group, 105 in all. Some forty-eight of them were described as gentlemen; there were twelve laborers and four carpenters; the rest were classed as servants, although they were really white slaves held in bondage for a limited period. It was in this settlement that money for the first time on the American continent replaced barter. Coins were few. The small store brought over by the immigrants were used only for the purchase of goods from England. These purchases were one-way transactions, since it was permissible to send coins to England but a serious offense to receive coins from the motherland.

The money used by the Jamestown colonists was tobacco. Its value was fixed on a pounds-shillings-and-pence basis and it was acceptable in payment of bills and debts—as much so as metal currency. It did not take long for the colonists on the Kennebec to learn of the new colony on the James River. Loading the *Virginia* with a cargo of dried fish and pelts, they set sail for Chesapeake Bay into which the James River empties. As they were without charts or a knowledge of the coast, the voyage was filled with terrifying adventure. Sighting Cape Charles and Cape Henry almost simultaneously one Sabbath morning, they entered the complex waterway of the Chesapeake and as if with a sixth sense found the mouth of the James River and its colony.

The meeting of the adventurers of the two colonies was an occasion of great rejoicing. Feasting and merrymaking ousted all thought of the business that prompted the expedition from the north. When the festivities ceased and the two groups of colonists got down to business, the men from the Kennebec who had lived by barter were stunned to find that all they could get for their cargo was tobacco, which none of them used. They could not exchange a single pelt for vegetables, fruit, corn, or any of the other commodities for which they had come such a long way.

When it was explained to them that supplies in the colony were for sale and not for barter, and that the tobacco money which they would receive in payment for the goods they had brought could be used to buy whatever goods were available, the men from the North saw the wisdom of the system.

During the return voyage of the *Virginia,* captain and crew discussed at length the advantages of the tobacco money as against their own barter system at Popham. The bleak climate, however, prohibited the growth of tobacco on the banks of the Kennebec and it was a 700-mile journey by sea to the James River. The captain, who had been deep in thought, spoke. "Men," he said, addressing the crew, "the good people of Jamestown chose tobacco plants as money because each plant is the result of so much labor. It is labor that gives it value. When they buy with tobacco, they are but giving so many hours of their labor for what they purchase." The men leaned forward, all attention.

"We have in Popham," the captain continued, "things as valuable and as convenient as tobacco."

The sailors looked inquiringly one at the other as they thought of their meager store of things they grew in the soil. "And what might they be, good master?" asked one of the men.

"Beaver skins!" shouted the captain. "There's not a man in our colony who has not a goodly store of them, for which he labored long and hard."

When the *Virginia* had returned after her adventurous voyage, her captain called the people of Popham together and told them of the use of tobacco money in Jamestown in place of gold and silver. He belittled the barter system and declared that articles necessary to community welfare should be valued in terms of money, which to them meant English pounds, shillings, and pence. Having no coins, they must have a substitute that in itself had value, like tobacco in Jamestown. The thousands of beaver skins stored in Popham were just the thing. Every skin represented hours of labor in hunting and skinning and curing the pelts. A prime beaver skin should be worth two shillings in any man's money, and as such should buy two shillings' worth.

The assembled colonists listened attentively. There was not one among them who had not, more than once, found himself on the wrong side of the bargain after a hard-fought barter. All of them had beaver skins in greater or lesser quantity, so it did not take them long to agree on establishing a workable currency.

A few years after this meeting of the colonists, a high-pooped ship cast anchor in a peaceful cove about 150 miles south of the Popham settlement. Wearied by their long voyage from England, passengers and crew came ashore and gave thanks for their deliverance from the perils of the sea, and for the bountiful land on which they had set foot. They were religious people, pilgrims in search of religious and political freedom.

When their ship, the *Mayflower,* had departed, and they found themselves confronted with the problem of sustaining life, they set to work with a will, hunting, fishing, and gathering edible roots, fruits and berries that grew plentifully in their new surroundings. Many of them had lived long in Holland and had learned the ways of ships and the sea. Some of them had Dutch coins in their purses on which was inscribed, "Our Way is on the Sea." Those built ships and reaped a rich harvest in the waters off Cape Cod. Others,

Russian fur buyers often ripped the buttons from their coats and used them as money when trading with the Indians.

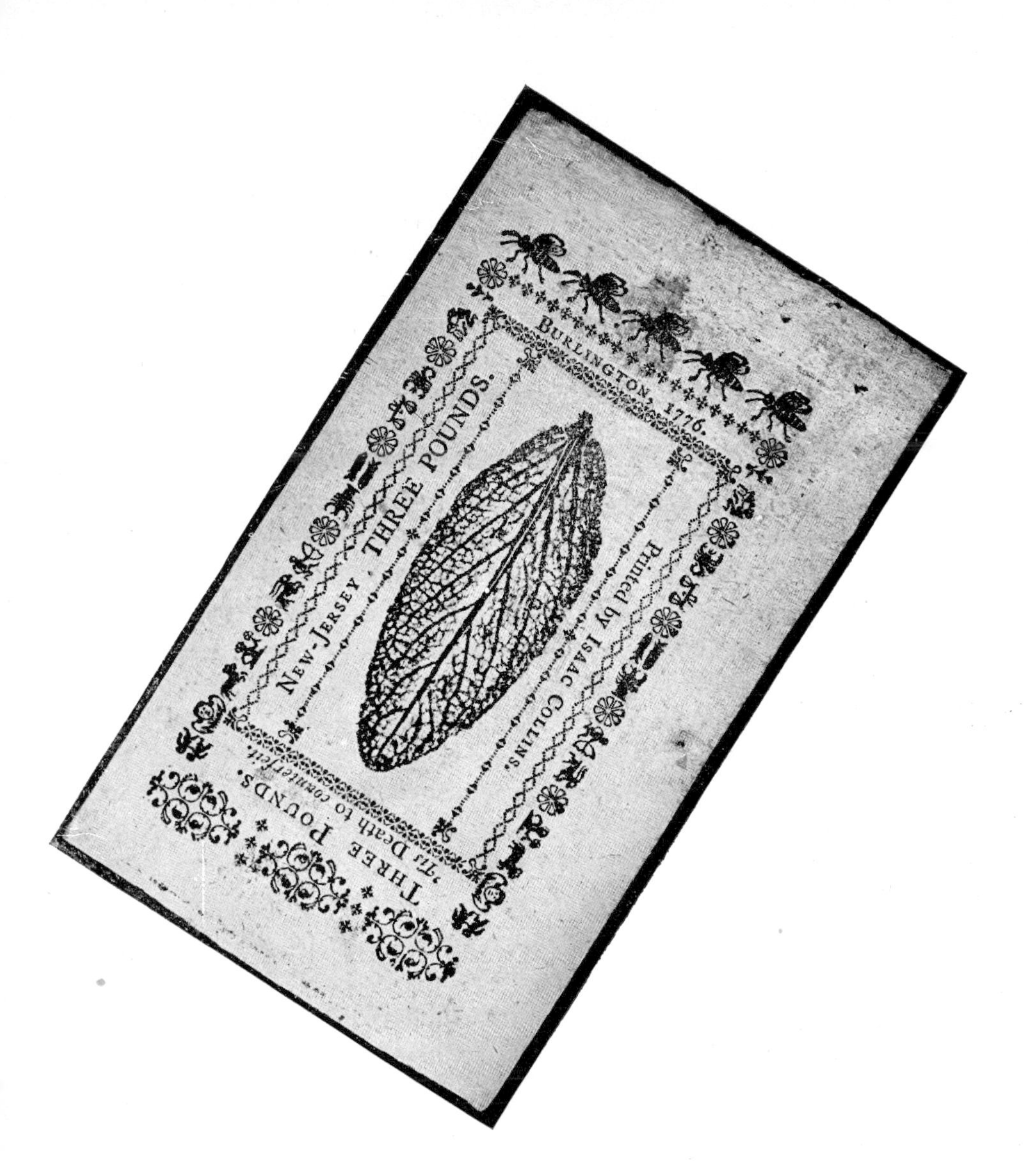

A colonial three-pound note issued in New Jersey. The influence of tobacco on the money of the period is indicated by the tobacco leaf. Note the signs of the zodiac at the top and bottom. The bees on the right symbolize industry. On the left is the warning, " 'Tis death to counterfeit."

who had lived by the soil, soon learned from the Indians the art of fertilizing the ground with their abundance of fish, and gathered bumper crops of maize and other grains. As these Pilgrims, by dint of work and community courage, forced security from the land and sea, and as other immigrants arrived and settled along the coastal area, an inter-community barter trade sprang up that resulted in the unequal division of worldly goods precisely as it had for thousands of years; the sharp bargainer waxed wealthy, and the trusting soul was left holding the empty bag.

One evening at sundown, a shallop rounded Cape Cod and sailed a leisurely course across the sheltered bay to where the Pilgrims had built the tiny settlement of Plymouth. As it neared the shelving beach and the word was spread that a vessel was approaching, the inhabitants, both men and women, crowded to the water's edge. A boat was lowered from the shallop and five men rowed ashore.

"A hearty welcome to ye, strangers!" shouted Robert Copper who had been mate on the *Mayflower*. "Come rest ye and be at home! Ye are Englishmen, I see!"

"Aye, English to the backbone—but not from England," replied the man at the steering oar. "We are from the Kennebec country, come to do some trading with ye."

It was from these men of the North that the Pilgrims learned the worth of beaver skins and how they could be used as money which, of course, was very scarce.

In spite of the hardships they encountered in their surroundings, the Pilgrims prospered. They built ships, cleared the forests and tilled the soil. As their number increased through new arrivals from the old country, they practiced many crafts, erected houses and places of worship and established villages here and there as they pushed farther into the wilderness. Their trade along the coastal area extended from Newfoundland to the James River. Occasionally some of the more daring crossed the Atlantic to England where they exchanged fish and furs and tobacco for commodities essential to their existence in America. These latter transactions were on a modified barter basis since they could not take money out of the kingdom.

In their dealings with people in widely separated localities, they were forced to use money of many kinds; dried fish, corn, bullets, nails, tobacco and, in some places, whisky. In the main, however, they found that three kinds of money were acceptable universally. In the northern area, beaver skins were the most desirable; in the south, tobacco was the favorite medium of exchange; and when dealing with the Indians, wampum was almost a necessity.

Corn, that is grain of any kind, and bullets were also a highly negotiable form of money. The former could be used as food, and the latter could be utilized in securing meat and, at times, as a protection against unfriendly Indians.

Of all the forms of this commodity money, beaver skins made the deepest impression on the country's economy. As late as 1788 the General Assembly of the State of Tennessee, then known as Franklin, enacted a law whereby the salaries of several of its members were to be paid in beaver skins, each of which had a fixed value of two shillings, or about fifty cents. For nearly a hundred years, the powerful Hudson Bay Company used beaver skins for buying or selling. A trapper sold his mink or fox pelts for so many beaver skins. When he bought food, or a rifle, or a number of traps, he paid for them with the same beaver skins. In the far Northwest, the vicinity of the Great Slave and Athabaska Lakes where beavers were most prolific, Indians paid as many as five hundred beaver skins, worth about $250, for disks of shiny copper to be used as shields. The early colonial courts imposed fines and penalties in terms of beaver skins, and continued to do so for many years after coins and paper money had been introduced. They had a valid reason for this. The early coins and paper money were looked on with suspicion by judges and people alike. A silver shilling might or might not be worth a shilling, but there was no doubt as to the value of a "beaver." In fact many persons refused government money and took skins instead.

In 1619, since tobacco was the dominant money in the Southern colonies, the General Assembly of Virginia passed a law giving tobacco a value of three shillings a pound. It also stipulated that all honest debts must be paid in tobacco, and further ordered that any person refusing to accept it as legal tender should be liable to three years of hard labor in prison.

At first the law was accepted by the people at its face value, until some legal mind discovered that there was nothing in the law to prohibit the voluntary use of coined money in payment of debts and other contracts. Two decades later, the General Assembly added teeth to the law by prohibiting the payment of all debts and contracts in anything but tobacco. The result was that everybody who owned or could lease a piece of fertile ground went into the business of planting and curing tobacco. Many a person who had lived in poverty for years thrilled at the sight of row on row of money sprouting from the earth. The large landowners went in for tobacco money raising in a big way. Great areas were cleared of forest and converted into tobacco land on which the rich loam yielded phenomenal crops. Before long storehouses, barns, and even kitchens were bursting with tobacco. Everybody had riches in tobacco money; there were no poor. Little by little it was discovered that in the rush to "raise money," other crops and even livestock had been neglected. The necessities of life—food, shoes, clothing—became scarce. A haunch of venison that formerly could be purchased for three pounds of tobacco, nine shillings, now sold for ten pounds of tobacco, or thirty shillings. A bag of corn meal, a plentiful commodity in the old days, increased its value thirty times; the price of other necessary goods jumped in proportion. Soon those with the most "money" were getting most of the available supplies; those with the more modest tobacco patches, who thought themselves rich, were disillusioned when they went to buy. In a short time tobacco money, which had been worth two shillings a pound (half a dollar) dropped to two cents and lower.

The good colonists of those days had never heard the word "inflation" used in the economic sense, yet they suffered from an acute case of it, brought on by a condition as old as time. When there is more money than there are things to buy, the value of money drops with a thud. That is inflation. The value of commodities does not rise; it is the price that goes up. A cut of meat sells for a dollar; that is its price. It will provide two meals; that is its value. When the same cut of meat sells a week later for two dollars, its price has doubled, but its value remains the same, since it still provides only two meals. When twice or ten times the price is paid for the same value, we have inflation. Conversely, when we pay half the price for the same value, we have depression. Inflation is father to depression, as the Virginia colonists learned to their sorrow. With

The shell money of the Indians, wampum, was often woven into useful and ornamental articles of dress.

tobacco money worth only two cents a pound as a result of too much tobacco, and with poverty in the midst of what was believed to be riches, petitions poured into the General Assembly pleading to have the planting of tobacco stopped forthwith, at least for a limited period. The Assembly refused to take action. "You cannot legislate people into prosperity," they said and let it go at that.

Depression in full flood swept the country. Desperate men, whose families were in want, gathered in groups and muttered their discontent. Hard words developed into harder action. The night skies of Virginia glowed red with the reflected light of burning tobacco fields, as bands of reckless men ranged over the countryside setting the torch to fields and sheds.

Alarmed at the wanton destruction, the Assembly met in 1684 and passed laws that put an end to the orgy of incendiarism. Whenever or wherever men in groups of eight or more were caught in the act of burning tobacco crops, they were adjudged traitors on whom only one sentence could be passed—death.

The crop-burning came to an end, but it was many a year before good times returned to the colonies in the form of the enhanced value of tobacco.

While the white men of the early days were working out their economic problems with beavers and bullets, tobacco and corn, the Indians were getting along nicely with a money system they had adopted long before the pale-faces set foot on the western shores. The redskins, following the custom that primitive peoples had adopted for thousands of years, wore their wealth as adornment. In this, they were not unlike some of our people today. Recently I was shown a string of pearls that had just been sold to the wife of a manufacturer of whom I had never heard. It was valued at $30,000. The oysters from which these pearls came differed only in shape from the shellfish from which the early Indians made the beads they used for money and called wampum.

Much of the shell money of the Indians came from the waters around New England and from Long Island, originally called by the Indians *"Seawanahka"* which means "the Island of Shells." These shells still abound in their early habitats. Along the shore in front of my house there are thousands of them still thriving and doing well in spite of present-day lack of value.

Fractional currency issued at different periods.

In this early shell money, the philosophy that money is a token of labor performed is well borne out. Only the spiral core of the shell was used for wampum. After the outer part of the shell had been broken away, the core was ground smooth and polished to dimensions of a quarter of an inch long and about the same thickness. I can vouch for the fact that this operation consumed an hour of labor, because I have tried it many times. This gives us an index of the value of the Indians' labor. Six wampum beads were worth an English penny, according to the Massachusetts rate of exchange in those days. Six hours of labor for a penny!

Just as we trade in terms of dollars, the Indians traded in terms of fathoms. A fathom was a string of beads six feet long containing 360 beads and valued at five shillings, or about a dollar in American money. There were slight fluctuations in value from time to time depending on how plentiful or scarce wampum happened to be.

Although the word wampum was derived from the Indian word *wampi,* meaning white, the beads were made from both black and white shells. Black wampum, as it was called, was really a very deep purple and had considerably more value than that made from white shells. The increased value was due to the fact that they were rarer; they were also much harder and, consequently, more difficult to grind and polish.

Many tribes wove the wampum beads into symbolic designs and used them on belts exchanged in intertribal treaties. Necklaces and broad collars of beautiful workmanship were also made of wampum and worn with ceremonial dress.

At first sight of the Indians' shell money, the white settlers smiled indulgently, as if at children playing with beads. The Indians, on the other hand, were astonished that the white men had no standardized money except beaver skins, furs, and corn, not acceptable to the red man because of his roving life. The Indians were the first to see a way out of the dilemma. "Why waste our valuable wampum," they reasoned, "when we can kill thousands of beavers and buy from the white man at will?" The colonists meanwhile followed the same line of reasoning. Since the Indians would not sell their venison, wild fowl, fruit and herbs for beaver, there was but one course open; they would go to the beaches and flats along the shore, gather shells and convert them into wampum.

The arrangement worked well for a while. The Indians, knowing the haunts of the beaver better than the white man, brought in prime skins that were not only acceptable, but valuable. The colonists, many of whom were skilled craftsmen, soon mastered the art of making wampum that was of better quality than that made by the Indians. So acceptable was the white man's wampum to the neighboring tribes that the production of wampum developed into an industry of considerable magnitude. Eventually the colonists adopted the shell money as their principal medium of exchange. They found it much more convenient than beavers, and quite as stable in value. Besides, the continued slaughter of the industrious little animals was bringing about a scarcity.

People in those days did not differ very much in their virtues or their weaknesses from those of today. Greed, the vice that had kept the world in armed turmoil through the centuries, was rampant in the colonies. Not content with taking the making of wampum out of the hands of the Indians, the lust for wealth prompted many to go into the business of counterfeiting. Inferior shells and clumsy workmanship characterized the mass production to such an extent that the debased shell currency soon dropped in value and was repudiated by many.

Meantime, the population of the colonies increased rapidly. Commerce expanded to the point where it outgrew the primitive money system. Local governments were established; order was springing from the chaos of the wilderness. Still loyal to the mother country, the colonists worked tooth and nail to build her empire. Stupidity in high places in the Home Government held out against providing the colonies with British currency. Coins of every kind were scarce. The meager quantity brought in by the immigrants was hoarded for the purchase of commodities that might be bought only in England.

Spain, on the other hand, had an extensive circulation of currency between the homeland and her colonies overseas. Spanish merchantmen ploughed the Caribbean and adjacent waters, then known as the Spainish Main. Their strongboxes were loaded to bursting with doubloons and pestoles and pesos, these last far-famed as "pieces-of-eight." The peso was a well-designed coin, about the size of our silver dollar, and about the same value, and was sometimes called the *peso duro* or hard dollar. Large quantities of these coins were

Pirate loot in the form of "pieces-of-eight" was often welcomed by authorities as a valuable aid to the meager currency of the times.

brought into the American colonies by ships trading in the West Indies. They were eagerly sought by the colonists, and used freely in their everyday transactions. Since other coins were scarce, it was difficult to make change when an amount of less than the Spanish dollar was involved. With American ingenuity, someone conceived the idea of cutting the coins into four parts. These, of course, were quarters worth about twenty-five cents each. Later the quarters were cut into "two bits," each with a value of about twelve and a half cents. The quarter of the Spanish dollar soon became known as two-bits, as is our present-day quarter of a dollar.

Much of the Spanish money used in the colonies in those days had been pirate booty before it was put into circulation. This, however, did not make it less desirable. Many a God-fearing merchant, to whom murder and rapine were unthinkable, enjoyed gleefully the jingle of the pirates' coins as they poured into his coffers. The Spaniards' ships were considered the fair and lawful prey of the freebooters, many of whom set out on their piratical forays armed with letters of mark bestowed by a Colonial Governor to whom a fat treasury meant more than high morals. Sir Henry Morgan, one of the bloodiest cut-throats that ever sailed the seas, was one of these pampered pirates. His sacking of Panama, his ravaging of Cartagena and the bloody swath of murder and pillage he cut through the Caribbean had the blessing and legal backing of the so-called authorities. L'Olonoise, Teach, Blackbeard, and scores of other reprobates of the period were all in collusion with the higher-ups ashore. From one cruise alone Morgan returned with more than a million and a half dollars in coins, jewels, and plate, to say nothing of vast booty in silks, spices and rare wines. The unwritten law of the pirates called for a division of the spoils among the crew, each man to his worth. Infraction of this law meant death, even to the leader.

Many of the communities along the seaboard profited hugely when the pirates or privateers, call them what you will, put into port. No sooner had mooring lines been made fast than the sea-rovers swarmed ashore to spend their share of the loot. The arrival of these pirate ships was always a major event in the lives of the shore-folk, for these men had clinking silver money and bags of jewels which they spent lavishly. Beaver, tobacco, and corn money were forgotten for the big disks of silver and the glittering trinkets, one-time gifts of Spanish grandees to their señoras and señoritas. Many of the maritime communities did a rousing business in repairs and supplies with the buccaneering craft. Game, fowl, vegetables, fruit and flour were purchased from whites and Indians alike. The pirates bought with an open hand. "Easy come, easy go," they said as they flung hard cash around like the drunken sailors they were. This pirate money seeped through the colonies in such quantities that it became an important item in the economy of the new country. Not all the coins in use, however, were of pirate origin. A lively trade between the colonies and the West Indies brought in a considerable amount of Spanish, French, and English money, although much of it was lost to the pirates in transit.

These windfalls of foreign money did not materially relieve the money needs of the colonies. The population was increasing rapidly and many necessities, and such luxuries as fine fabrics and old wines could be secured only in England and France. This import business, done on a strictly cash basis, periodically drained the colonies of coin currency.

Many petitions sent to the Home Government in England for permission to set up a mint in Massachusetts invariably brought a curt refusal. Desperate at seeing their trade strangled and their commerce starved, the good New Englanders cast caution to the winds and, in defiance of the mother country, set up a mint. That was in 1652 and in that year were struck the first North American coins. They were a poor job of minting and proved a miserable failure. Made only in the denomination of one shilling, and struck from soft silver, they were crude in design and workmanship. On one side was stamped N.E., the initials of New England, and on the other XII denoting the value in English pence. The edges were unmilled, that is, they were perfectly smooth. That was a fatal error since it encouraged coin clipping. It is strange that in stern religious New England one of the oldest and most pernicious rackets of the Old World should spring up overnight.

As soon as the new shilling appeared, the unscrupulous ones in the community gathered up all they could lay their hands on, and began whittling slivers of the soft silver from the edges of the coins. The amount taken from any one coin did not seem very much, but the parings from a hundred showed a handsome profit. As the

The fugio, designed by Benjamin Franklin, was not a popular coin. It was soon discontinued.

coins passed from hand to hand, they became smaller and less valuable, until they were no longer suitable for currency. This New England shilling proved a sad adventure, but taught the colonists many things about the art of minting.

Having defied the Crown without disastrous results, the Massachusetts Assembly decided to go a step further and issue new and better made coins. These were put in circulation—a shilling, a half-shilling or sixpence, and a quarter-shilling or "three penny bit." These proved more successful and were soon followed by other issues, the latest of which was the famous "pine tree shilling," so called because of the pine tree it bore on one side.

Some time after the issuance of this coin, a British official, just returned from the colonies, laid before his king—Charles II—several of the pine tree shillings, remarking that the colonies were getting out of hand by defying the law and minting their own money. The king, who knew little about such affairs, but who had a fanatical belief in the loyalty of his subjects, went into a violent rage. That Englishmen across the seas should defy their king was unbelievable.

One of his close advisers, Sir Thomas Temple, who was present, endeavored to pacify the infuriated monarch. Sir Thomas was a man of quick wit and lots of common sense.

"May I look at one of the coins, Your Majesty?" His voice was low and unruffled. The king flung the shillings on the table.

"Take them!" he shouted, "and see that something is done about them."

Sir Thomas picked up one of the coins and examined first one side and then the other. A smile rippled across his face. "Your Majesty," he said humbly, "perhaps we are mistaken as to the intent of these good people. It seems to me they are doing honor to Your Majesty."

"Honor?" exploded the king. "Faugh!"

Unruffled by the interruption, Sir Thomas approached the king and pointing to the pine tree on the coin purred, "You will notice, Your Majesty, that they have placed on the coin the Royal Oak, under which Your Majesty's life was saved, as a memorial to your deliverance. They are loyal Englishmen indeed."

The king took the coin and examined it. His wrath gave way to a smile. "You are right, Sir Thomas," he said. "The Royal Oak it is. Let them mint to their heart's content. They are honest men."

And mint they did. One by one, each of the colonies brought out its own issues, and began to enjoy in a small way the benefits of an established metal currency designed and minted for its own particular purposes.

This independent coinage in the colonies disturbed their opponents in London. It was established, however, and little could be done about it except replace it with coins minted in England for colonial use. Patents were granted to William Wood of London, authorizing him to mint coins for the American colonies. In due time, the new issue was sent overseas, and was received by the colonists with gratitude since their supply of coins from all sources was far from adequate for their needs. Wood, a sharp businessman, learning of the scarcity, sold to the colonies an issue of coins he had minted for Ireland, but which had been refused by the Irish because of poor workmanship. Even these were gratefully put into circulation in an attempt to ease the coin stringency.

The coinage in use in the colonies at this time was a conglomeration of coins from many countries—English shillings, French louisdors, Spanish doubloons and pieces-of-eight, to say nothing of the local coinages.

Meanwhile, the old reliable beaver, wampum, and other commodities continued to serve as money for the rapidly growing communities. Members of the Assembly of Franklin were paid for their services at the rate of three raccoon skins a day. In many places a Justice's fee was one mink skin.

About that time, in 1785, the Congress adopted the dollar as the unit of our money and, at the insistence of Thomas Jefferson, introduced the decimal system as the method of reckoning. Two years later, in 1787, Benjamin Franklin, much concerned with the monetary famine, devised a coin he called a "fugio." It was of small denomination, made of bronze and highly symbolic. In fact, it was the first one-cent piece. On one side was represented the sun, casting its rays on a sundial, under which was a typical Franklin admonition, "Mind your business"; the other side was bordered by an endless chain of thirteen links representing the unity of the original thirteen colonies, and in the center was the simple statement, "We are one."

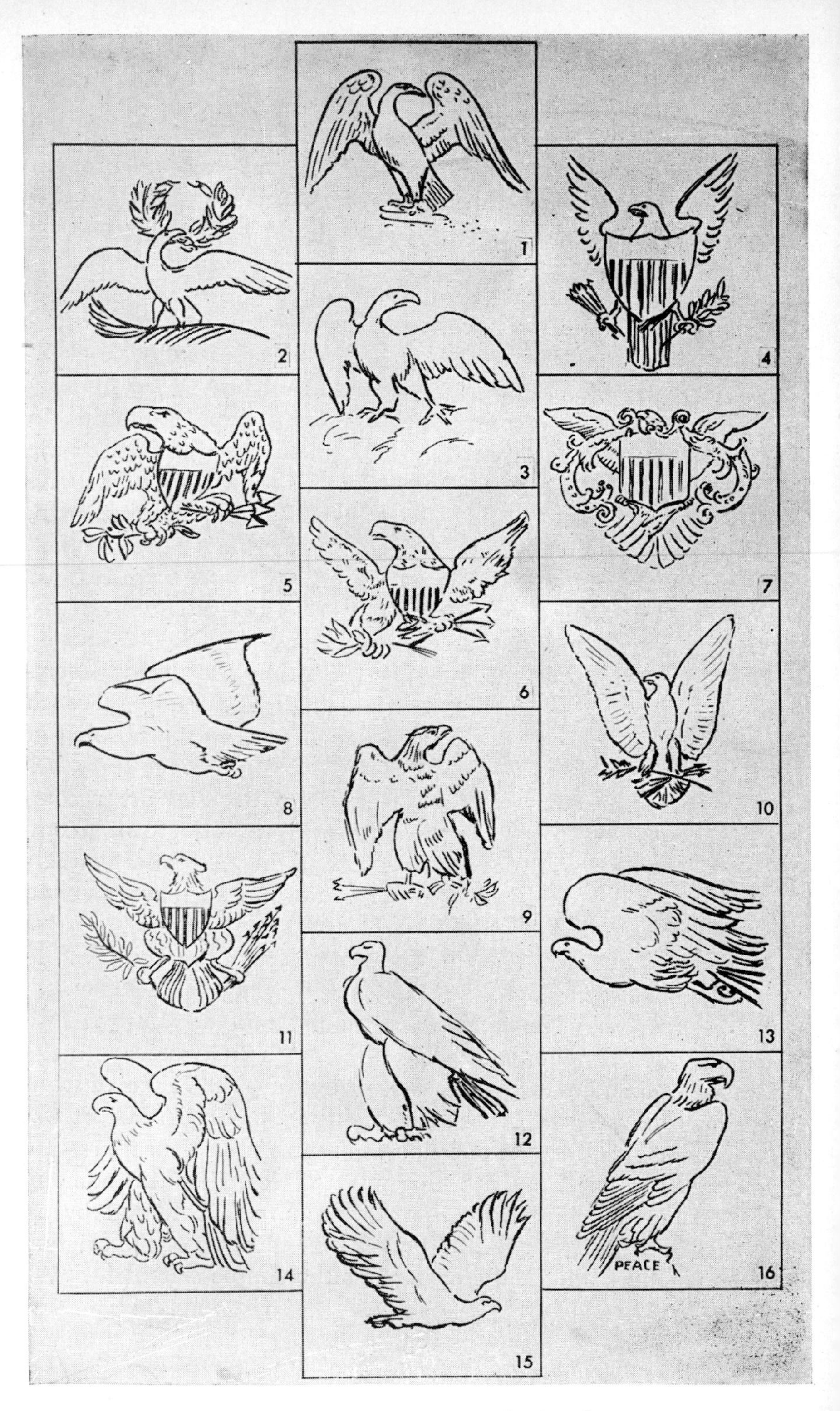

Showing the development of the American eagle on our coins since the earliest days.

The name fugio, however, did not have a popular appeal and there was much controversy over a suitable name. It was Governor Morris who hit upon the word "centum," Latin for hundred, meaning one-hundredth of a dollar, and who later shortened it to "cent."

It was not until 1792 that the United States established a monetary system of its own, and set about the task of minting its currency. A United States mint was opened in Philadelphia under the first Director of the Mint, David Rittenhouse.

Rittenhouse must have felt like a boy who has been given a set of carpenter tools, but who had no wood on which to use them. He had all the mechanical equipment for turning out a stream of metal coins, but he did not have a scrap of metal, nor even an order to begin coining. Rittenhouse, a Philadelphia Quaker more interested in serving his country than in the high-sounding title of Director of the Mint, went to see President Washington and explained his dilemma.

"Here I am, Mr. President," he said, "the duly appointed Director of the United States Mint without so much as an ounce of gold, silver, or copper to make the coins the country needs so sadly!"

"Do not fret, good Rittenhouse," Washington replied, "you shall have silver a-plenty and soon."

That evening, as Washington sat down to dinner with his wife, he cast his eye over the gleaming silver on the table and sideboard. Much of it had come from England, and many of the finest pieces had been fashioned in Boston by a patriot who was a gifted silversmith, Paul Revere.

Never loquacious, Washington was almost silent during the meal. Martha, his wife, a woman of great understanding, knew that some affair of state was weighing heavily on the President. She, too, remained silent.

When they had finished the meal, contrary to his custom Washington leaned back in his chair, still in deep thought. He picked up a silver spoon from the table and studied it, weighing it in his fingers. "Martha," he said abruptly, "there's nigh on a dollar's worth of silver in this spoon."

The astonished wife replied, "There is at least that much silver in it. It is one of our best. Would you prefer that we use the service that came from France?"

The President smiled. "No, good Martha, it is the silver, not the service, that interests me. At this moment our country needs silver more than it needs tableware. The mint has not as much silver as there is in this spoon to make the currency we need so badly."

The next morning a two-horse dray pulled up at the entrance to the mint and unloaded a heavy chest addressed to Rittenhouse. When the Director of the Mint saw its contents, he gasped. It contained tableware and tea-services, vases and candlesticks, all sterling silver, and on each piece was engraved the Washington crest, or coat-of-arms. Rittenhouse had acquired the silver with which to begin the operation of the United States Mint.

The first coin to be made of the Washington silver was a half-dime. This was made at the President's suggestion, for soon after its issuance, he said in his address to Congress, "There has also been a small beginning in the coinage of half-dimes, the want of small coins in circulation calling the first attention to them."

The new coin, notwithstanding the generous gesture of the President and his wife, was not a success. It was so small in size and light in weight, it failed to impress the people favorably. In fact, much of the issue was distributed by Washington among his friends and acquaintances as a souvenir or lucky piece. It fulfilled its purpose, however; it stimulated Congress to purchase more than 150 tons of copper for coining into cents and half-cents for which there was great need.

Three years after the issuance of the Washington half-dime, the United States Mint went into coinage in a big way. The country was in sore need of a stable and convenient currency. People were tired of the makeshift custom of using the currencies and denominations of other countries.

In 1795 the United States coined its first silver dollar. It was modeled after the Spanish piece-of-eight, for many years the most popular coin in the colonies. The name "dollar," however, is of Bohemian origin and came into being in a curious way. In that picturesque country there was a fertile valley, the patron saint of which was Saint Joachim. In time the valley became known as Joachimsthal, meaning the dale or valley of Saint Joachim. Here were located the rich silver mines owned by the Counts of Schleck. The silver from those mines was of unusual purity. At the head of the valley a town grew up and that, too, was called Joachimsthal. It was not unusual in those days for a prosperous community to issue its own money. Having plenty of silver of great purity, the good people of Joachimsthal coined with a lavish hand; they struck coins that were large and fine and called them "Joachimsthalers." This was soon shortened to "thalers." Because of the quantity and quality of the silver in these coins, they were eagerly received by the European countries. As the Bohemian "th" was pronounced "d" in Scandinavian and Danish, the "thaler" was called "dalar" in those countries and was, consequently, called "dollar" in England. Soon the term dollar was applied, particularly in the colonies, to the Spanish piece-of-eight because of its size and the fineness of its silver. And so it was that our unit, or standard coin, a fine generous well-minted piece, was called a dollar.

Our phrase, "the Almighty Dollar" dates back to the Joachimsthaler. So generous was its weight and fine its quality, and so eagerly sought was it, its purchasing power was such that it was called "Almighty." It was Washington Irving who gave it its present connotation when he wrote of the "almighty dollar" as "that great object of universal devotion throughout the land."

And so, in summing up the subject, we have learned that the chief reason for the use of coins as money is their convenience. Oxen and sheep, and skins and tobacco were all very well in their day when they were the only substitute for the barter that men practiced unsatisfactorily for so many centuries. They were, however, at best inconvenient and cumbersome mediums of exchange. The backwoodsman who journeyed to the trading post to buy a musket was forced to carry a pile of beaver skins almost as tall as himself to pay for it. Some years later after coins had been introduced, he had but to carry a small buckskin bag of coins inside his shirt to make a similar purchase.

It is this convenience, among other things, that also prompted the use of gold. A twenty-dollar gold piece is less than half the size of a single silver dollar, yet is worth twenty of the larger coins. If coins were to be used in a thousand-dollar purchase, it would take about three pounds of gold coins to consummate it, while it would take about sixty pounds of silver coins. Where large sums of money were carried, it is not surprising that gold was preferable to silver. Where very small amounts were concerned, however, copper or bronze was preferable. Five cents in gold or one cent in silver would be so small that it would be almost useless as a coin.

Confederate hundred-dollar bill, issued at Richmond, Virginia, in 1863.

Five-dollar note issued by the Madison and Indianapolis Railroad by authority of the General Assembly of the State of Indiana in 1843.

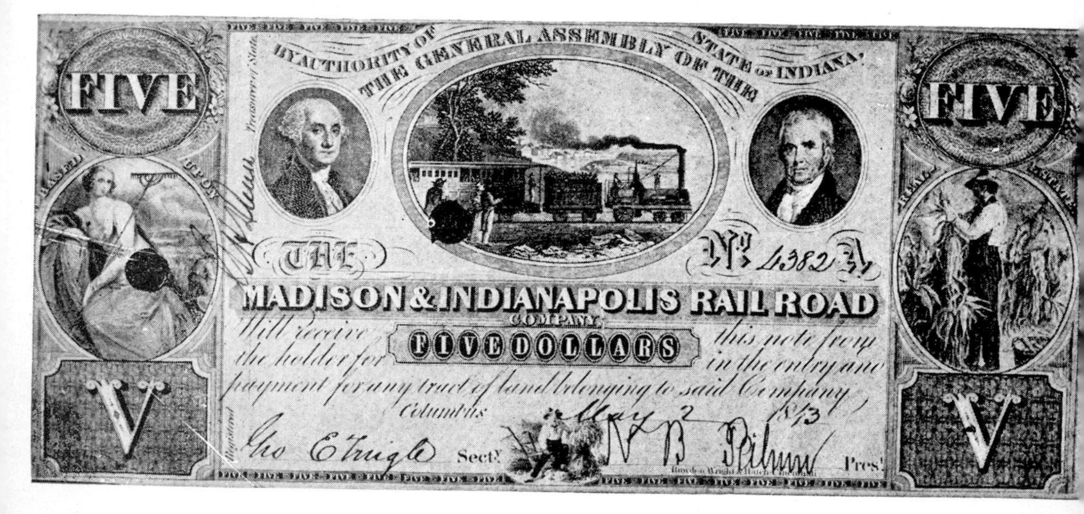

4

Convenience or portability is also an important reason for the use of paper money. A thousand-dollar bill can be carried as easily as a calling card, while its equivalent in silver would wear out a strong man in a very short time.

Of course, its portability is by no means the only reason for its existence. For instance: suppose a thousand-dollar bill were accidentally dropped on the street, and was whisked by a gust of wind into a sewer, and was eventually carried out to sea, only the owner would suffer a loss. The wealth of the country would remain unchanged since the bill, in itself, had no more intrinsic value than a paper napkin. The gold or silver for which it was only a kind of receipt was still secure in some vault. It is, in fact, called the "security" that is behind paper money and coins of small denomination.

The first paper money of North America was issued in Canada in 1685. With funds from France long overdue, the colonial government was unable to pay the troops. The soldiers were already

SHACKLES OF PAPER

growing surly, and ominous rumors of mass desertions and worse reached the Governor. As the weeks passed, the morale of the men became lower. Violence had broken out on several occasions. To make matters worse, the weather was bitterly cold and food was none too plentiful.

While things were at this crisis, the Governor made a tour of the garrison to see for himself how the men were taking their hard lot. It was an informal visit. The pomp and circumstance usually attending an inspection by the Governor were laid aside. In a corner of the barracks room, a group of men were engaged in a card game in which they used torn cards as counters. The Governor observed that the players were as keenly anxious to win the pieces of pasteboard as if they had been louisdors. He left the garrison deep in thought.

That evening, he astonished his aide-de-camp by ordering the seizure of all playing cards whether in the garrison or elsewhere. When the cards had been collected from soldiers and colonists alike, the Governor issued a proclamation ordering that playing cards duly signed by him should be accepted as currency—according to the value written on each one.

Any money was better than none to the soldiers and colonists. They accepted the playing cards gladly, and began to spend them at once.

In all the world, there was no thriftier soul than the French colonist in Canada. To possess money was his great ambition, yet he had none; he had lived by barter. When the playing-card money was issued, he cherished it as if the cards were sheets of gold, for had not *Monsieur le Gouverneur* guaranteed them with his signature? Then a strange thing happened. One day, many weeks after the issuance of the playing-card money, several chests of silver coins arrived from France. The Governor issued another proclamation to the effect that all playing-card money then in circulation would be redeemed in good hard silver. The counting room at the Governor's mansion was ready for a rush of people anxious to receive silver in exchange for their pasteboard money, but no one came. Days passed and only a few asked to have their cards redeemed. Then a peremptory order went out *demanding* the return for redemption of all playing-card money. This seemed only to

A three-pound note issued in the Colony of New Jersey during the year in which the United States was born.

increase its popularity. Failing to understand it, the government accepted the situation. It brought out several large issues of the card money, thereby contributing much to the economic happiness of the colonists. So successful was the cardboard money that some sixty-five years later the then existing issue was increased to one million livres or about $200,000 in United States money. By a strange coincidence, no better form of backwoods money could have been devised; it was tough, wear-resisting, convenient in size and was almost impossible to counterfeit.

Five years after the Canadians had issued their playing-card money, the American colonies found themselves in the same straits that had forced their neighbors to the North into the issuance of playing-cards as money. Coins were scarce, in some places non-existent. Even commodity money was difficult to obtain in quantities large enough to enable them to carry on their commerce. Massachusetts was drained dry by an ill-advised military sortie into Canada. Her soldiers had not seen money in months. Disgruntled and growling, they became a menace to the peace of the colonies. At a meeting of the General Assembly there was a unanimous demand that something be done, and quickly. It was agreed to print an issue of paper money in denominations as low as five shillings and as high as five pounds.

There were few in the colonies that ever had seen paper money; therefore, it was difficult for them to attribute value to the insignificant looking scraps of poorly printed paper. A beaver skin had at least intrinsic value; so had corn, tobacco, bullets and the other commodities they had been accustomed to using as money. Even the Indian wampum had established value and was a first-class substitute for coins. They hesitated to sell the fruits of their labor for a scrap of paper; in fact, many of them refused the notes as payment for their goods. So strong was the feeling against the newfangled paper money, the government was forced to come to its rescue. In 1692, the Assembly passed a law making the paper money receivable for taxes and at a premium of five per cent over and above silver.

It was this five per cent that eventually doomed the issue. Counterfeiters saw easy money in manufacturing these bits of paper that were worth a hundred times their weight in silver. Printing presses were at a premium, and engravers could name their own price. Counterfeit notes were sold by thousands at a fraction of the face value of those issued by the government. The genuine notes were crude and of poor workmanship. Neither the paper, nor the design on it had any protective devices, so that the outlaw engravers and printers had no difficulty in making passable imitations. Before long the colony was flooded with the spurious notes, with the result that the genuine became almost worthless.

Notwithstanding the disastrous experience of the people of Massachusetts with paper money, Pennsylvania some years later took a flyer in paper notes that got the instant approval of the people. Profiting by the experience of the Bay State with the counterfeiters, the Pennsylvanians used their notes as a medium to convey a message to the lawless that counterfeiting would not be tolerated. On every note was printed in bold type the line "Counterfeit is Death."

The warning, however, was not worth the paper it was printed on. Counterfeiting flourished; counterfeiters were arrested. Some were executed; others had both ears cut off and were sent out into the world as living examples of the administration of justice. Many were fined $100 and were condemned to pay double the loss of those to whom they sold the spurious notes. In extreme cases the counterfeiter was sold into slavery for seven years. Yet, in spite of the severity of the law, the illegal money-makers did a land office business. Paper money seems to have held its own, thanks to the precautions of the government.

In 1729, Benjamin Franklin, then about twenty-three years old, published anonymously a brochure entitled *A Modest Inquiry into the Nature and Necessity of Paper Currency*. In it, he appealed to the government of Pennsylvania to enlarge the paper currency. His effort was successful. Years later he admitted the authorship in his *Autobiography,* in which he told how the popularity of his pamphlet among the common people overcame the opposition of the wealthy Philadelphia merchants, and caused his proposal to be carried by a large majority in the House. "My friends there," he wrote, "who considered I had been of some service, thought fit to reward me by employing me in printing the money, a very profitable job and a great help to me."

An example of fractional currency—actual size—issued by the United States government in 1866.

Subsequent events proved that Franklin, notwithstanding his attainments as scientist, statesman, and philosopher, was not a sound economist.

During the above period, the use of the printing press in the creation of money became epidemic. The New England colonies, as well as New York and New Jersey, turned out a deluge of notes which depreciated rapidly until they were worthless. In Connecticut it took 118 paper dollars to purchase a silver dollar's worth of goods. In Rhode Island, where paper currency was strenuously opposed by merchants, businessmen and the more intelligent people in the community, the multitude clamored for more and more paper money; it provided an easy way of paying old debts. Even public debts were paid in money right off the printing press. Public works were carried on and paid for by a few dollars' worth of paper. Pennsylvania built a jail and paid for it in bills bearing a picture of the ugly building, later known as the Walnut Street Prison.

With paper money flying around like leaves in an autumn wind, there was but little silver or gold to back it up. The exports of the colonies, chiefly hides, furs, and tobacco, were less in value than the English goods imported for consumption. This left the colonies owing considerable sums, a condition known as an *unfavorable trade balance*. The deficiency had to be made good in gold and silver; consequently, each colony in turn was drained of its specie, or coined money. As it is impossible for any trading community to exist without some medium of circulation, the colonies, one by one, turned to paper money, making it fulfill as far as possible the functions of gold and silver. Some communities, realizing that paper unbacked by security of intrinsic value was worthless, used land as collateral. Franklin preached the doctrine that notes issued on money security were money, so bills issued on land as security were *coined land*.

Based on Franklin's doctrine, a land bank was opened in Massachusetts. It issued 35,000 pounds, English money, in paper notes, or as they called it "coined land." In several cases banks were opened that made loans in paper money on real or personal security.

Chaos grew. No man knew from day to day how rich or poor he was. Colonial Assemblies bequeathed their debts in paper money to their successors, who in turn ordered new issues without redemption value. Tom Paine, author of *The Rights of Man,* wrote, "This kind of paper money is the illegitimate offspring of Assemblies, and when their year expires, they leave a vagrant on the hands of the public." In 1749, it was said that owing to the depreciation of colonial notes, every honest man not in debt had lost about half his personal estate.

The first upturn came in 1750 when the English Parliament made a grant of silver money to Massachusetts. Steps were taken immediately to redeem the depreciated paper at the rate of seven and a half shillings of paper for one shilling of silver. The result was like that of a blood transfusion; the patient rallied, business picked up, industry took a new lease on life and an almost forgotten prosperity was felt. The West Indian trade enjoyed by Newport, Rhode Island, passed over to Boston as Massachusetts became known as "the silver money colony."

Unfortunately, none of the other colonies followed suit. The period has been spoken of as "the carnival of fraud and corruption." The groundwork for one of the great financial muddles of history had been laid.

Relations between the colonies and Britain had gone from bad to worse. Ominous war clouds hung over the colonies, bringing fear and uncertainty. Conflict seemed inevitable at a time when the Continental treasury was almost empty. In 1775 the Continental Congress, too timid to tax, resolved to finance the coming war by issuing paper money with the faith of the colonies as security.

It was decided also that the bills of such an important issue should be of the finest workmanship, so as to discourage counterfeiting. A Boston silversmith, who had made something of a name as a fine craftsman, and who was known as a stanch patriot, was given the order to engrave the necessary plates. He was Paul Revere, whose famous ride became epic.

Nominally the bearer of this paper money was entitled to receive its face value in Spanish milled dollars, or their equivalent in gold or silver; to get it, however, was another matter. Within a year six million dollars in paper had been issued. Twelve months later thirteen millions more had been added. The inevitable happened. In less than two years the paper money lost half its value, yet the colonies could not decide on taxation. Most of them made no effort to meet the cost of the war either by assessment or contribution. The printing press was thought to be the only recourse. It was worked day and night, turning out scores of millions of dollars.

Obeying the economic law, the credit of Continental paper continued to sink lower and lower. Thomas Jefferson computed that the one hundred and forty million of paper dollars issued in 1779 had a value of less than seven million dollars. Two years later the paper dollar was worth a little more than a cent, and soon after became practically valueless. It took 20,000 Continental dollars to buy a beaver hat. Barbers took up the practice of papering their shops with the discredited bills and so helped coin the phrase "Not worth a Continental."

To add to the confusion, debts might be legally paid in the worthless money. Stories went the rounds of creditors leaping from windows to escape debtors attempting to pay them in Continental currency.

The Continental Congress and the individual States, frustrated by the public's refusal to accept the depreciated money, tried unsuccessfully to bring about a change. In 1776 Congress passed a resolution declaring that any person who refused to accept paper money should be treated as an enemy of the country and deprived of all trade intercourse. Arrests and jail sentences were numerous, and many lesser culprits were obliged to make public apology.

It is difficult to imagine what would have happened to the economic life of the infant republic at that time, were it not for commodity money. A beaver skin or a pound of tobacco was still as good as gold and as stable in value. Skins and furs of certain animals were also considered as negotiable as silver or gold. The Governor of Franklin, later Tennessee, received one hundred deerskins as salary. Five hundred deerskins were paid "His Honor the Chief Justice." The County Clerk was awarded three hundred beaver skins and the Clerk of the House of Commons received for his services two hundred raccoon skins.

After the Treaty of Peace with England in 1783, affairs in the newly formed republic entered a period of still greater confusion. Although the limited supply of hard money available was sent to Europe in payment for arms, munitions and other necessaries of war, it was not enough to pay our creditors in full.

Fractional currency.

In spite of the commercial chaos and the desperate condition of public finance, Washington took up the job of rehabilitation without a qualm. Providentially he had available two men of giant intellectual stature on whom he could lean—Thomas Jefferson and Alexander Hamilton. Not until the new Constitution had passed the Convention, and the first Federal Government was established under Washington was it possible for the United States to establish a national system of finance. The Constitution empowered Congress to coin money and regulate its value. Furthermore, it deprived the States of the right to coin money, issue bills of credit, or make anything but gold and silver coin legal tender in payment of debts. The framers of the Constitution had turned thumbs down on the old paper money system and the people, still licking financial wounds inflicted under the old regime, hailed their deliverance.

Their troubles were not yet over. After organizing the Treasury Department and the first Bank of the United States, Hamilton set about building a new financial structure from the ground up. With Jefferson, he held out for the decimal system as superior to the British system then in use. He ordered from the Mint issues of ten-dollar eagles, half-eagles and quarter-eagles, all gold. Of silver, he ordered issues of dollars, half-dollars, quarter-dollars, dismes (dimes) and half-dimes. The copper coinage was to consist of cents and half-cents. The proportional value of gold to silver in all coins was to be in the ratio of fifteen to one—that is, fifteen ounces of pure silver had the same value as one ounce of pure gold.

The new and sound coinage acted at once as a powerful stimulant on the people. They went to work with a will and did not stint their effort, for now a man was paid a dollar for a dollar's worth of labor and with that dollar he could buy a dollar's worth of food or clothing. Prosperity, after a fashion, began to return. The future looked bright.

Suddenly it was discovered that the Mint failed to provide sufficient coinage for the needs of the country. The result was that foreign gold and silver coins were made legal tender in order to make up for the deficiency in hard money. Then, to make matters worse, our gold coins gradually disappeared from circulation. When there was practically none left, it was discovered that the gold coins had been undervalued. This was too good an opportunity for other countries to miss. They bought up our entire issue and made a handsome profit in the transaction. Then our full-weight silver dollars gradually disappeared under an avalanche of clipped and worn Spanish and Mexican silver dollars. So deadly was the onslaught of the depreciated foreign silver, the American Mint suspended the coinage of silver from 1806 to 1834.

Meantime, the paper notes that had virtually disappeared from circulation were again making an appearance under conditions that caused their rapid depreciation. As a result of the financial mess, Congress refused to renew the charter of the first Bank of the United States, but failed to correct the disorders of the metallic money or the hopeless depreciation of paper money.

Again war came in 1812, and with it the heavy financial load it imposes on a country. President Madison's declaration of war against Britain was followed by the suspension of specie (coin) payments. Overnight every printing press in the country was put into service, grinding out paper money, most of which was not worth the ink with which it was printed. In 1814, Secretary of the Treasury Dallas wrote, "The multiplication of State banks in the several States has so increased the quantity of paper currency that it would be difficult to calculate its amount and still more difficult to ascertain its value."

In the hope of remedying the evils that had stunted the healthy development of our financial system, a second Bank of the United States was created in 1816, with a provision that it could not issue notes of less than five dollars. This, too, proved futile, for in less than two years an orgy of wildcat banking spread through the States. Looseness of management, lack of legal regulation and, in many cases, outright swindling made the public jittery. Soon banks began to topple, business came to a standstill, payments in coin were suspended and, once more, panic gripped the country.

The financial seesaw continued its ups and downs. When the crest of the panic had passed, a slow recovery began that continued for nearly fifteen years and culminated in what at first looked like prosperity. In an effort to hold the gain the country had made, Congress refused to renew the charter of the second Bank of the United States. This was hailed as good news, since many believed that most of the financial woe of the past had its source in that institution.

The action of Congress was followed immediately by a tremendous expansion of State banks. Newly opened lands in the West, a rapidly growing shipping industry, and an upswing in manufacture and commerce brought on an outburst of wild speculation. Local banks were hastily organized to reap a rich harvest from the promised profits. Borrowers had but to ask for money with no thought of security. Investments in worthless land and fly-by-night enterprises followed. People who had been in want a year or two previously now had their pockets filled with paper money which they squandered at every turn. Prices of commodities soared to new heights. An intoxication of spending had gripped the country. For every dollar's worth of goods on sale, there were ten dollars ready to buy it.

Inflation does not subside; it bursts like a boiler under excessive pressure, wrecking everything within reach of its explosive force. Overnight the country found itself prostrate in the grip of depression. Hard times had come again and remained for ten years.

In 1849, while conditions were still bad throughout the country, a miner picked a gold nugget from a California stream and unconsciously let loose another outburst of inflation. Rightly or wrongly, it was generally believed that the scarcity of gold was responsible for the recurring financial fiascos. As rumors of the untold riches in the hills of California spread eastward, men and women flocked to the land of gold in covered wagons, sailing ships, afoot and on horseback. Of the thousands that reached the gold fields, few attained the wealth they had anticipated, and even those sent back glowing accounts of the fortunes that were being made with the aid of a pan and shovel. These stories were so exaggerated as they were passed along that a gold fever seized the country. Fraudulent banks sprang up like mushrooms, particularly in the western states.

An orgy of wildcat speculation again broke out and printing presses worked overtime turning out forged bank notes. It was said that more than five thousand kinds of fraudulent bank notes were in circulation. During this insane era of inflation, prices of commodities and services rose to fantastic proportions. In California where gold was plentiful and commodities scarce, eggs sold for a dollar apiece, flour was $60 a barrel, boots brought $50 a pair, a breakfast of ham and eggs cost $6 and the laundress who did not make $15 a day considered herself poorly paid.

In 1857 the bubble burst, and starvation and suffering followed, particularly in the Middle West. Banks flickered out like street lights at dawn. In New York and New England, where a sounder system of banking had been established, most of the banks weathered the storm.

The young country was gaining its experience in the vagaries of finance the hard way; but learn it did, little by little. Under the National Banking Act, passed in 1863 to assist in financing the Civil War, every bank issuing notes was required to deposit with the Treasury, United States bonds as security. This, at least, restricted and regulated the indiscriminate issues of paper money that had made a shambles of the financial structure so often over so many years.

Again, as in all wars from the days of Caesar, the huge problem of paying the soldiers bedeviled Lincoln and his government. As a first step, specie (coin) payments were suspended and paper money known as "greenbacks" was issued. The greenback got its name from the color of the ink used on one side of the bills. Again the fear of taxation won the day and the painless process of paper money was adopted. The circulation of greenbacks was eventually confined to the National banks and for the first time a national system of paper money had been established in the United States.

The paper currency of the Confederate States ultimately became valueless, while the greenbacks, although they depreciated to less than half their gold value, recovered and were restored to par or normal gold value in 1878.

When the government suspended specie payments in 1861, postage stamps were used extensively as small change. To further relieve the condition brought about by the shortage of coins, corporations, banks and small tradespeople flooded the country with small paper notes. These tiny bills, called "shin-plasters," caused a tremendous confusion and were driven out when the government minted great quantities of fifty-cent pieces, quarters, dimes, and nickels.

In the years that followed, controversy on "sound" money was endless. Presidential elections were won and lost on that issue. Supporters of gold fought it out with adherents of silver. Periodic inflations were followed by panics, more lately called depressions. Money had become a commodity as well as a token of work done. As a commodity it was bought and sold like cotton or wheat. Speculation, gambling, and often double-dealing were accompanied by drama and tragedy. Newspaper headlines spoke of "The Wolves of Wall Street" and of the public as the "Shorn Lambs." Industrialists often followed the daily stock quotations more anxiously than the production charts of their factories. Bootblacks and bankers, magnates and minor employees kept one eye on their jobs and the other on the stock-market ticker. It was estimated that in 1929 nearly twenty million people were involved in stock speculation, carried away by the thrill of paper riches.

About that time a friend of mine, who formerly had been an industrious man, sat with his wife on the beach in front of the Casino at Deauville, France. An hour previously he had received from his broker in New York a telegram congratulating him on having his profits on stocks reach the million mark that day. For

So limited was the coinage of the United States in 1844 notes were issued for 10 cents.

nearly a year, he had devoted all his time to playing the stock market. Now he was enjoying a needed rest at one of Europe's most fashionable seaside spots.

"And now, my dear," he said to his wife, "shall I wire my broker to cash in, call it quits and hold what we have, or shall we go after another million?

After a long discussion they decided to continue gambling while luck was with them. He cabled his broker to buy heavily of a certain stock. Two days later while the new-made millionaires were in Paris, the financial world was convulsed by the cataclysm of October, 1929. Within a short time the paper million had vanished like a morning mist, and my friends found themselves worse than penniless—in debt.

While speaking with them later, after the crash, the husband said to me, "Anyone who gives up working for a living to take up gambling for a living, is beaten before he starts."

During the inflationary period prior to the 1929 slump and, indeed, during the ten-year depression that followed, paper money proved itself as stable as coin currency. Until it was decided to conserve our great supply of gold by going off the gold standard, a ten-dollar gold certificate could be exchanged in any bank for a ten-dollar gold piece. A silver certificate then as now was worth its face value in silver. We had at last learned our lesson in the proper way to use paper money.

In perusing the earlier part of our financial history, one might attribute the inept handling of our financial affairs either to stupidity or to downright political greed. It was neither the one, nor the other. It was purely the result of inexperience, not only with the intricacies of money, but with the foreign money manipulators who had had centuries of practice in financial juggling and who saw easy picking in the young republic.

Our legislators and bankers were, in the main, simple forthright men but they were wholly provincial when it came to dealing with "furriners." Many of them lacked education and few, very few, had ever been outside the confines of the country they loved so dearly.

The economic philosophy of those men was a simple one. They drew a sharp distinction between money and wealth. The forests, the mountains, the plains, and the oceans that washed the shores teemed with wealth. It took only work to convert that wealth into money. The forests that grew to the water's edge gave them timber for the finest, fastest ships that man had ever built. The fertile soil grew grain in prodigal abundance. The mountains and the hills yielded rich ores. From a short stretch of the New England shore, whalers put to sea and brought back in one year more than $6,000,000 in oil and whalebone. The wealth of the nation was measured in tons or bushels or barrels, not in dollars or pounds or marks or francs.

Those men did not fear for the financial future of the United States because they had the resources that enabled them to *earn* the money necessary to the country's welfare. The ups and downs and ins and outs of currency were often disagreeable episodes that came and went like floods in the spring. With each crisis they learned something of value; they gained experience. Even while these financial rashes covered the economic body, they pioneered and built, worked and sweated. They made mistakes as they went, just as all humans do. Conservation did not occur to them. They

Wooden nickel issued at Blaine, Washington, during financial crisis of 1933.

squandered their resources on land and sea, almost to the point where bountiful nature could not replenish the waste. Here too they learned, little by little. Their errors were errors of commission, rarely of omission. Their credo was "Action," their slogan, "Do it now!"

As the republic grew and took its place among the older nations as a power in world affairs, it still held to its philosophy—"Natural wealth plus work result in financial strength." It saw competitor nations reach out the arm of conquest and scoop riches into their coffers—the taxes of enslaved peoples. It saw the money marts of the world shuffle and reshuffle their golden hoard and turn the tide of fortune in their favor, or as often happened, against their neighbor. At home and abroad it saw greed and avarice among those who would get something for nothing, who through gambling and wild speculation gathered in money that represented financial manipulation rather than work performed. It suffered the torments of internal war and politico-religious differences, and yet it did not waver. It was a large family with family squabbles, but also with a determination to build family security through toil and sweat, come what may.

Our American doctrine of "work and win," while it has never been disputed, has of recent years been misunderstood by a large segment of our population. We often hear the expression, "workers and management," as if our population were divided into two groups, those who worked and those who, because of their supervisory capacity, did no work. This fallacy is further emphasized in the classic fiction, "labor and capital," a favorite newspaper phrase.

All workers can be divided into two categories, physical and intellectual. The physical workers, usually called "help" or "hands," might be likened to the enlisted men of our armed forces. The intellectual workers are the commissioned officers, responsible to the men under them and to their country for the success of the military venture. The first essential of this success is the fullest co-operation and co-ordination between the commissioned and non-commissioned groups. Discord, slackness, or shirking on either side would mean certain defeat. To preserve fighting power, the officers must acknowledge the value of the men who do the physical fighting, and the enlisted men must acknowledge the value of the officers who do the intellectual work of directing the operation.

The man who punches the time clock finds it difficult to credit the boss, who comes and goes at will, with giving to the business in which both are engaged as much physical and nervous energy as he does. He does not realize that the time clock is a meter that measures out his daily working hours with the accuracy of a gas meter. The boss has no such device to check his working hours. In that most of his work is mental, he toils at his job every waking hour, and it is a known fact that heavy and continued mental work will wear a man out more quickly than physical labor. The executive side of all business carries with it a burden of worry, and every worker knows that his daily job, no matter how heavy it may be, is light compared to the worry over, say, a sick child at home.

Recently I visited an industrial plant. At the end of the day shift, the president invited me to ride home with him in his automobile. Near the entrance to the plant we picked up three of the workers to give them a lift. They were three fine strapping young men, well dressed and well fed. During the drive they discussed heatedly the day's baseball scores. After a while, I noticed the president was fast asleep.

When we had dropped the workers at their respective corners, my host apologized for his nap. Then I learned that he had spent the preceding day until late at night in Washington where he was engaged in a battle for priority of certain vital materials. No sleeping accommodations on the train, he had sat in a coach until five o'clock in the morning. On arriving at home, he had changed his clothes and left immediately for the plant where he put in a trying day until four-thirty in the afternoon.

That evening there were guests for dinner, among whom were two of his younger executives and their wives. After coffee my host and his associates adjourned to the library, where they discussed a vital change in plant routine until midnight. After the dinner guests had gone—I was an overnight guest—my host apologized again, explaining that the plant in which several thousand persons were employed had been saved from a shutdown. So fatigued was he, he scarcely realized that the dinner was in celebration of his sixty-first birthday, or that it had been forty-two hours since he had lain on a bed.

Such extreme cases of self-imposed endurance among members of management are by no means unusual, particularly when the drums of war beat in our ears. On the other hand, there are innumerable cases in which the man at the bench, or desk, or loom, or oil derrick has thrown aside all thoughts of personal comfort and labored without stint until a crisis had passed. In no country on earth are the men who do the physical work and those who direct industry so close in their ideals.

Despite press reports of labor troubles, the number of workers involved is insignificant when compared with the vast army of men and women loyal to their jobs and their country. It has been estimated that less than one-twentieth of one per cent of labor man-hours is lost through labor trouble. That is the equivalent of one worker losing three minutes in a hundred working hours.

It is on this basis of work, combined with our natural wealth, that the United States has amassed its riches. The vagaries of finance and the legerdemain for better or worse of our financial geniuses

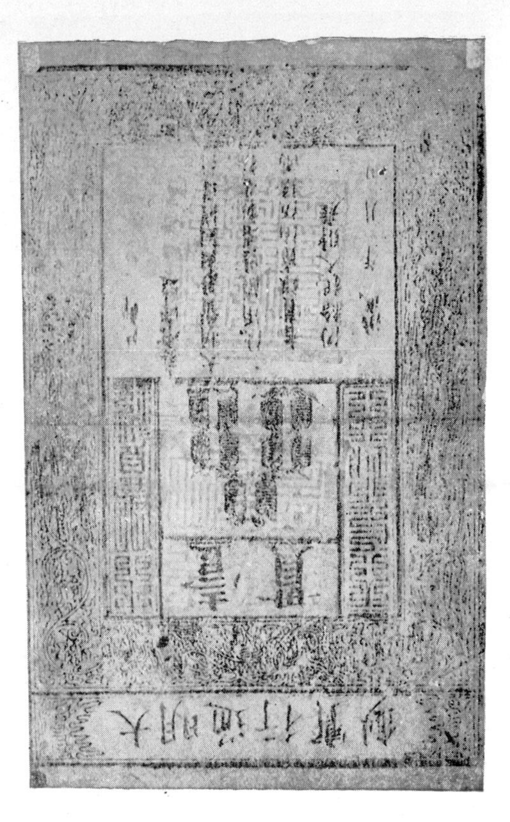

This is the mulberry paper money of which Marco Polo wrote. Issued by the storied Kubla Khan, it introduced many reforms into early Chinese currency.

were and are only minor incidents in the great drama of development. In the earth and the sea and the air are capital on which we draw. From the sweat of human endeavor come the dividends in gold and silver, to say nothing of human achievement that has made us the richest nation on earth in less than a hundred years.

The steam engine, the cotton gin, the sewing machine, the telegraph and telephone, the automobile, the harvester, the airplane, the electric light, the cinema, and a hundred other aids to man's productivity came from the brains and sweat of Americans, and with them came the golden reward of work.

Practically in every case, these milestones of human development were set firmly by men whose boyhood was spent in humble surroundings. Edison, the Wright brothers, Henry Ford, and the others attained financial success not through genius alone, but through genius combined with work—hard, unremitting work.

This modern structure houses the U. S. Mint at Denver, Colorado.

5

THE MINT, MOTHER OF MONEY

HIGH AMONG the gods and goddesses of early Rome stood Juno, the consort of Jupiter. A fine figure of a woman, tall and statuesque, she was protectress of all womankind. The men of ancient Rome paid homage to her, also, and regarded her as the guardian of finance. So deep was their devotion, they erected a temple to her in 344 B.C. and called it the temple of Juno Moneta, or "Money Juno." It was in this temple that many of the finest Roman coins were produced, and from Juno's surname Moneta comes our word "mint," meaning a place where money is manufactured. The early mints were crude affairs; in fact, they were little more than glorified blacksmith shops in which brawny men wielded heavy hammers all day long.

The crudity of the early coins was largely responsible for much of the money troubles of the world. Long before the Lydians or the Chinese invented coins, gold and silver were precious metals that stirred men's cupidity. In those early days there was no public store of gold or silver. Each man had his private hoard which he guarded constantly against the forays of bandits or the pilferings of servants.

When coins of gold and silver were introduced, those who sold their labor, or the fruits of their labor, found themselves for the first time in possession of greater or lesser quantities of the valuable metals. It was theirs to do with as they chose—beat it into ornaments, bury it in the ground, or give it in exchange for something they needed or fancied. If, they reasoned, a small part of each coin is removed by scraping, the receiver will be none the wiser and the payer will get what he purchases, saving a little of the magic metal into the bargain. The idea spread like oil on water and was soon practiced in every country where coins were used.

As the crude coins passed from hand to hand, each owner scraped his little share from it so that at the end of a month or a year each coin was considerably lighter than when it left the coiner's anvil. When the coins reverted to the royal treasury, through taxes, levies, or contributions, the government found itself short-changed by the good people for whom it issued the coins in the first place.

Laws carrying heavy penalties for the coin-clippers were enacted. Torture, mutilation, and death were inflicted on the culprits without appreciable effect on the wholesale robbery of government money metal. As the coins became smaller, to the point where they were no longer acceptable as currency, some unknown but clever rascal introduced a new technique for robbing the coinage. Placing a quantity of coins in a leather bag, he shook and churned them violently for hours on end. When he tired, his wife lent a hand and often passed the treasure pouch over to the children to continue the grinding process. The new method, while more laborious, had the advantage of removing the metal, not only from the edge but from the face of the coin as well. When a sufficient quantity of the metal had been pilfered from the coins, the bag, now thoroughly impregnated with tiny particles of gold or silver, was burned and the ashes placed in water. The ashes floated away, the heavier metal dust, sinking to the bottom, was recovered and melted down to be sold either in bulk or as counterfeit coins.

This practice, known as "sweating," was carried on for centuries, and was introduced into early America by immigrants, particularly those from central and southern Europe.

Before the new coins are delivered to the Cashier of the Mint, they are weighed in the boxes in which they are packed. This is known as a weight check against count.

New and more stringent laws were passed and banishment was added to the penalties. The long arm of the law, however, found itself powerless to curtail the activities of the clippers and sweaters. It was found then, as it has been learned many times since, that people cannot be legislated into the path of righteousness.

So great was the quantity of gold and silver stolen from coin currencies, financial crises arose with alarming frequency.

National evils never occur singly. Each brings others in its wake. As the cankers of clipping and sweating progressed and full weight coins became scarcer, another criminal cult slipped in. The members were known as cullers. Their method was to collect coins in large quantities, often through loans, culling out the full weight coins, melting them down, and exporting the metal ingots to other countries at a large profit. They repaid their loans entirely in lightweight coins.

The English parliament worked overtime formulating and passing laws against clippers, counterfeiters, and the rest of the money-hungry horde that preyed on the coinage. Sentences of death, imprisonment and branding were meted out right and left. Wagons loaded with offenders charged with crimes against currency were hauled up Holborn Hill in London, the public execution place. One spring morning seven men were hanged and one woman was burned at the stake for coin-clipping, but without stemming the tide of lawlessness.

Many of the clippers were said to have made large fortunes. One, an old offender, offered £6,000 or $30,000 for a pardon. Although his offer was rejected, the fame of his riches spread from one end of the country to the other and counteracted the deterrent effect of his hanging. It is a curious fact that an otherwise law-abiding person considered coin-clipping a perfectly respectable occupation, tinged perhaps with adventure. While all knew that the injury done by the clippers as a class was enormous, each individual act of clipping was looked upon as a trifling transgression. Even during a financial crisis brought about by the petty pilfering of gold and silver, those hanged for bringing it about had popular sympathy. Constables winked at the offenders, justices were hesitant to commit them, witnesses refused to give testimony and juries, except in flagrant cases, brought in verdicts of "Not guilty."

Comparable to coin-clipping, in its devastating effect on a country's finance, was the debasement of coins as practiced by the rulers who controlled the coinage.

About the time the United States was emerging from its colonial status, Adam Smith whose *Wealth of Nations* became a sort of international textbook on economics, wrote, "In every country in the world the avarice and injustice of princes and sovereign states, abusing the confidence of their subjects, have by degrees diminished the real quantity of metal which had been originally contained in their coins . . . By means of those operations, the princes and sovereign states which performed them were enabled, in appearance, to pay their debts and fulfill their engagements with a smaller quantity of silver than otherwise would have been requisite. It was, indeed, in appearance only; for their creditors were really defrauded of a part of what was due them."

The debasement of coins followed two patterns. The royal purse snatcher who owed a million florins, minted coins from silver to which he added, let us say, twenty-five per cent of valueless base metal, thus cheating his creditors of a cool quarter of a million florins. The second method of royal pilfering lay in issuing coins of pure silver and reducing their weight by making them thinner and of slightly smaller diameter. These coins were further depleted by the clippers and sweaters until they were no longer acceptable as currency.

It remained for James II to go the other royal pilferers one better. When that shifty monarch had been ousted from the English throne and had fled to Ireland, he found himself shy on cash while heavily burdened with debt. Ordinarily, those noble debtors lost little sleep over the plight of their creditors. James, however, was confronted with establishing an expatriate government and raising an army of his own. At that time Ireland enjoyed the doubtful benefits of British money. In the city of Dublin, where many of the merchants were English, trade was brisk and a comparative prosperity was enjoyed by its people. One of James' first acts caused tradespeople and customers considerable alarm. He issued a proclamation that all the old brass in the country must be turned in to His Majesty's scrap pile. The brass drive went on for months. Pots, pans, door knockers, old cannon, even brass buttons then popular, poured in from all quarters. Severe penalties awaited those who failed or refused to comply with the monarch's order.

It was generally assumed that the collected brass was for use in casting cannon and other implements of war. James had other ideas, however; he was secretly converting the metal into shiny brass coins. At the appointed time, the worthless coins were poured into circulation. A royal edict was issued, declaring the brass pieces to be legal tender "in all cases whatsoever." A value sixty times greater than their intrinsic worth was given them.

When the pretty new coins appeared, there was consternation among the businessmen and rejoicing among the counterfeiters and the public, who saw a chance to pay off their debts painlessly. A mortgage for a thousand pounds could be paid off by a bag of the coins made of old kettles. Creditors and mortgage holders who complained to the king's Court of Chancery were told to "take their money and be gone!"

The shopkeepers suffered most. To protect themselves, they raised the prices of their goods, whereupon the magistrates promptly clamped a price ceiling on all merchandise.

Anyone possessing the new coins was privileged to walk into a shop, lay on the counter a piece of brass worth a few pennies, and walk out with goods more than sixty times its value. There was no legal redress for this systematized robbery. The soldiers, long without pay and half-starved, now finding themselves with brass money in their pockets, pounced on the bakers' shops like a swarm of locusts. Some of the more daring of the merchants refused the spurious coins, and were promptly hauled before the Provost Marshal. Immediately, they were cursed as traitors to the king and threatened with hanging in their own doorways. Some were thrown into dungeons and held until all resistance to the plague of brass money had broken down.

In medieval times debasement of the coinage was almost universally practiced by European governments. The French kings were notorious offenders. King John of France, known as "John the Good," kept the currency in a continuous state of confusion from which he profited greatly. John's virtues were external ones. He committed his peculations in secret with the aid of his coiners who were sworn to secrecy under pain of death.

Molten metal being poured into ingots to be used later for five-cent pieces. Photographed at the Philadelphia Mint.

During the Seven Years' War, Frederick the Great, finding himself in serious need of money, called in a coiner named Ephraim, and commanded him to counterfeit the fine silver thaler then in use. The counterfeits were made of copper with a plating of silver on the outside. When the war was over, the king restored honest silver coinage.

When Elizabeth I reigned, there lived in England a man of great wisdom where matters of money were concerned, Thomas Gresham by name; he was a successful merchant and founder of the Royal Exchange. When a boy he was apprenticed to his uncle, a London dry-goods merchant. Later he was admitted to the Mercers' Company, an association of dry-goods men. So astute was he in business, he was appointed to the post of "king's merchant" in Antwerp. The good Queen Bess, always on the lookout for able men, took notice of Gresham's sagacity. She knighted him, and dispatched him to Brussels as her ambassador. Some time later he appeared before the Queen and propounded to her what later became known as "Gresham's Law." It was to the effect that *bad money always drives out good money*.

The Queen, always a little stubborn in her ideas, argued hotly that the good can always drive out the bad. Then Sir Thomas patiently explained to her the simple economics embodied in his law. "Your Majesty," he said, "if yonder handmaiden went out to buy a bonnet at a cost of a golden guinea, and in her purse were two golden guineas, one of them good and of full weight, the other clipped and sweated to the value of several shillings, yet both had the same purchasing power, which guinea would she offer in payment?" The Queen pondered a moment, "If she were a scrupulous wench, she would pay in good gold." The royal reply had a touch of acid in it.

"You are right, Your Majesty," said Sir Thomas bowing low, "but in all Britain from John O'Groats to Land's End there are not, of wenches or men, a corporal's guard whose conscience would prick them to such honesty."

The Queen, a clever woman, saw in Sir Thomas no mean adversary in a discussion. "But what of the mercer of whom the wench bought?" she asked shrewdly.

"He, too," replied Sir Thomas, "will match the good with the

Before the newly made coins leave the U. S. Mint, they are given a bath in a kind of washing-machine known as a "tumbler."

bad and give in his commerce with others, only that of lesser value. The good he will save for a better market."

In spite of Gresham's Law, which became known in every money mart in the world, inferior coins continued to drive out good money. Once introduced, debased money became a highly infectious monetary disease that always resulted fatally. It stopped at no boundaries, but spread from country to country, killing off the weak quickly and dooming the strong to eventual collapse. This, America learned to its sorrow many times before it grew strong enough to stand on its own financial feet.

From the earliest days of coinage the counterfeiter has been a menace to the stability of money, and it has taken the utmost vigilance of the governments of the world to keep him under control. More than once he has tipped the delicate financial balance on the side of disaster.

For many centuries the penalty for counterfeiting was death, sometimes in terrible form. The crime was particularly malignant since it was aimed at the ruler, universally considered the sponsor of the country's money. In spite of the severity with which the illicit coiner has always been treated, he has carried on his outlawed trade with more or less success. Even today the United States Secret Service, under the administration of the Treasury Department, carries on an unrelenting war on counterfeiters. Yet, notwithstanding the hawklike watchfulness of the Treasury agents, counterfeit coins and counterfeit bills still find their way into circulation in the United States, although the volume of such spurious money has declined sharply in recent years. There is little chance that this spurious currency manufactured by reckless nonentities can ever be more than a national annoyance.

On the other hand, it is entirely possible that an unfriendly nation, possessed of the skill and mechanical facilities for the production of counterfeit money, might attempt to destroy our money structure by the circulation of such quantities of "queer" money as to cause confusion and possible panic; this, of course, only as a war measure intended to break down public morale. The Secret Service is on guard against any such attempt.

Coining money is, at best, only a manufacturing process carried to a high state of perfection. It is in that perfection that the safety of coinage lies. The counterfeiter, no matter how skilled he is, or how complete his mechanical equipment, can never hope to make a coin that is a true replica of a standard piece turned out by the Mint. In the first place, if he uses gold or silver at all, it is heavily loaded with an alloy; the more alloy, the greater his profit. This brands his coins as spurious even to the uninitiated. They lack the musical ring of the genuine; they are lighter, softer and in some cases have a greasy feel. Secondly, the workmanship is inferior to that of coins issued by the government. The dies and molds of the counterfeiter are usually made from the genuine coin. To the eye of the expert they are at once discernible as "phony."

Although coin counterfeiting is as old as money itself, the counterfeiter has made little progress in the development of his art. I saw seized counterfeit appliances recently that were almost identical with those used in the Middle Ages. From the earliest times, gold has been the coiner's first choice of all the metals and no substance that could adequately replace it has ever been discovered. Silver has been second choice. These metals, more than any others, possess the many technical characteristics necessary to good coinage. They are uniform in substance, so that coins of equal weight will always have the same value. They may be melted down and coined and recoined any number of times without appreciable loss. They are durable in value. Although they may increase or decline over a period of years, they have had a high standard of value for thousands of years and at no time has history recorded that their worth depreciated below the point where they were considered precious. They are highly impressible; that is, they receive the impression of a die with great fidelity. This is most important, since it is essential that a coin be recognized instantly and be easily distinguished from counterfeits.

In coins of lesser value, copper has been the most successful. It is well adapted to coinage in that it takes a faithful impression. It may be melted and used over and over; it is also easily distinguishable and wears well. Like gold and silver, it is mixed with an alloy the amount of which is determined by law.

All United States coins are produced by the Bureau of the Mint, whose administrative offices are located across the street from the Treasury Building in Washington. The Bureau might be likened to the home offices of a large manufacturing concern with plants located in widely separated cities. The factories of the Bureau, called coinage mints, are in Philadelphia, Denver and San Francisco. It also has assay offices in New York and Seattle. These might be termed laboratories and stockrooms, for in them the precious metals are weighed, tested, and analyzed for fineness, then stored until required. At Fort Knox, Kentucky, and at West Point, New York, are located what might well be called the nation's gold and silver storage warehouses—huge depositories in which ingots of gold and silver are piled like bricks to the tune of billions of dollars. It is because of these stock piles of precious metals that a ten-dollar bill will buy the same amount of food or fun as ten silver dollars, something practically unknown to our forefathers.

The coinage, although developed to a high state of perfection, differs little in principle from that used for centuries. In fact, some of the early Roman coins made with crude equipment, compare favorably with some of our best coins in use today. Although we lack details of the various steps of early coinage, it can be safely assumed that all coins had their beginning in a sketch of the design made by some accomplished artist. When the sketch was approved, an engraver reproduced the design on the end of a cylinder of iron, steel, or bronze, called a die. Dies were engraved for the obverse and reverse sides of the coin. The obverse die was set in an anvil, and a disk of metal was carefully placed over it. The reverse die was placed on the disk while a coiner held it in position with tongs. When the uppermost die was struck a heavy blow with a sledge hammer, the image on it was impressed on the upper side of the metal disk, while the image of the lower die was forced into its lower side. That is all there was to it. The process was slow, however, as coins must be made singly.

As need for larger issues grew, the speedier method of casting was adopted. The original die was reproduced many times in the form of molds. Several molds could be set up at once and molten metal poured into them. The process was so simple that counterfeiters saw in it a rich harvest. All they needed was a coin from which to take the impression and the proper material for the molds. This method of casting coins is still practiced by counterfeiters. It requires no great skill and little equipment. Compared

The old and the new. Note similarity between the early steam coining press and the super modern electric coining press.

with our beautifully stamped coins of today, the cast counterfeits are so crude that they fool none but the most careless or the most ignorant.

It is an important duty of all citizens of the United States to defend the integrity of our currency. The counterfeiter is a public enemy, a criminal who preys on both our government and our people. Uncontrolled, he is capable of doing great damage. The United States Secret Service wages war on him day and night. Without the aid of the police and the individual citizen, the battle would be a losing one. Any person, young or old, can take a hand in the fight if, upon receiving a counterfeit coin, he reports the circumstance to the police or to the nearest Secret Service office. Spurious coins can be detected in any one of five ways—If a counterfeit coin is dropped on a hard surface, it gives off a dull metallic sound; the genuine has a cheerful clink not unlike a bell. Nearly all "phony" coins have a greasy oversmooth feel, something like satin as compared with taffeta. If examined under a glass, the corrugated edge of a genuine silver coin shows the little ridges to be absolutely even and regular. On the counterfeit these ridges are uneven and without sharpness; they are usually rough and badly nicked. Counterfeits are usually made of soft metal and can be pared with a penknife easily. The genuine gold or silver coin has been hardened by the slight addition of an alloy and is difficult to cut. The old expression "the acid test" had its origin in the centuries-old war on counterfeiters. The most unerring of all the tests is the application of a drop of silver-test acid to a suspected silver coin. If the coin is counterfeit, its metal will turn black where the acid has touched. If it is a genuine silver coin, the surface remains unchanged.

The counterfeiter and coin-clipper received their first major defeat during the reign of Charles II in England when coins were made by machinery for the first time. The sledge-hammer and the hand-held dies were abandoned for a screw press capable of exerting many times the power of the hammer even when wielded by the most muscular of hammer-men. Under the irresistible pressure of the screw, the soft metal, gold or silver, was not only forced downward but outward against a circular collar on which was engraved a grained pattern or a short legend. This left an embossed surface on the rim of the coin that showed clearly any attempt of the coin-clipper to pare off the edge. It also increased the difficulties of the counterfeiter by making casting more difficult. The first "mill and screw," as invented by Benvenuto Cellini, was hand operated. Then a horsepowered machine was built and used for many years.

About the end of the eighteenth century a coin press, operated by steam power, was set up in England by a private firm. So excellent was the work done by this private mint, several foreign governments negotiated with the owners for installations of similar machines.

The first American silver dollar was made in the new United States Mint at Philadelphia in 1795. It was not a beautiful coin but it was an honest one, so honest in fact that it was eventually gobbled up by the domestic and foreign money sharks.

Since those early days the art and craft of minting have come a long way. In contrast with the puny hand-presses of Alexander Hamilton's time, the modern coin-making machines as used in the United States Mints are marvels of power and precision. Every step in the development of these mechanisms has made it much more difficult for the counterfeiter. At the same time every improvement has expedited the manufacture of the vast pile of coins necessary for use in our daily cash transactions.

During World War II, no nickel or bronze coins were made. The five-cent piece was made of an alloy of copper, silver and manganese. The one-cent piece was zinc-coated steel.

To keep the wheels of business moving, nine hundred million dollars in coins have been placed in circulation. This means about $6.75 in the hands of every man, woman and child in the United States. This huge sum is merely the small change necessary to supplement our paper money of which there is more than sixteen billion dollars in use.

When the money metal arrives at the Mint, it is usually in the form of bars which, when built into piles, look like shiny bricks. Now begins a series of weighing operations in which each bar is checked for weight to the fraction of a troy ounce. The bars are also assayed for purity. The copper or other metals that are added to make the coinage alloy are also weighed with extreme accuracy.

Let us assume that a batch of half-dollars is to be minted. The process is something like this: The silver and copper in proportion set by law are placed in a crucible and melted and mingled until they become a homogeneous mass. The chief function of the copper is to improve the wearing quality of the silver which is exceedingly soft in its pure state. After the molten alloy is poured off into molds, it comes out in the form of ingots. The ingots are trimmed to remove rough edges and hollow ends, then are assayed to make sure they contain the legal proportion of silver and copper.

The next stage in the manufacture of the coins is rolling. The bars are squeezed flat between rollers until they are a certain width and thickness and take the form of sheets ever so slightly thicker than the coins that will be made from them. The sheets are passed along to a "trier," who tests their thickness with a sensitive gauge and punches from them disks known as "trial blanks." Again the scales are used; the blanks are weighed with greatest accuracy. If any are found too light or too heavy, the sheet of metal from which they came is sent back for re-processing. Even after the sheets, or "fillets" as they are called, have passed the trier, they are again punched and weighed. The scrap metal remaining after the blanks have been punched out is known as "clippings" and is also sent back to the crucibles for re-melting.

When the blanks are approved, they are put through an edge-rolling machine that, by compression, makes the edges somewhat thicker than the blanks. This has a twofold purpose; the thicker rim or edge protects the face of the finished coin from wear; and it also enables handlers of large numbers of coins, as in banks, to stack them more easily.

The edged blanks are now ready for the presses, where they are fed accurately into position, resting on the lower die and enclosed snugly in a steel collar on the inside of which is the "reeding" or corrugations that will be on the edge of the finished coin. The upper die now descends on the metal blank under many tons of pressure. As both dies squeeze the metal blank between them and sink into its soft surfaces, the alloy, being ductile, is forced with great pressure toward the sides and into the corrugations of the collar. The dies separate almost instantly and the finished coin is pushed out to make way for the next, and so the operation is repeated about a hundred times a minute. The coining procedure is the same for all coins, regardless of their denomination or the metal from which they are made.

So meticulous is the government in making our coins beyond reproach, that the finished coins are reviewed. Any imperfect coins are condemned and re-melted. The good coins, as a further precaution, are again assayed before they are approved finally as currency.

As I have said, the money of a country is merely a quantity of tokens or markers for the work done by its people in converting its natural wealth into the things that make for better living. In spite of the vicissitudes through which our currencies have passed since the days of our forefathers, those charged with the handling of our national money have been ever faithful to the trust placed in them. Being human, they made errors. But their honesty and their patriotism were beyond question.

Bowed by the crushing financial problems brought on by the Civil War, and despondent over its debilitating effect on the country's resources, Secretary of the Treasury Salmon P. Chase wrote the Director of the Mint, stating that no nation can be strong except in the strength of God, and instructing him to place on our coins the motto, "In God we trust." A two-cent piece was the first to bear the words that may be found on our coins to this day.

As the coins are struck, they are inspected as they pass over an endless belt. Defective coins are remelted.

Composite of Hamilton's head from a counterfeit and genuine ten-dollar bill. On the left of vertical dividing line, the counterfeit engraving is blurred and uncertain. On the right it is clean and sharp, showing the superb workmanship on a genuine bill.

6

Authorities may disagree as to whether the Chinese or the Lydians were the first to coin money, but it is generally conceded that the rulers of China were the first to establish a system of paper money. As early as the ninth century A.D. business transactions were carried on more or less successfully in China with the aid of paper notes. There is evidence that nearly three hundred years later, the country, swamped under a flood of depreciated and counterfeit paper money, entered a depression that lasted nearly a hundred years, leaving poverty and untold suffering in its wake.

The Mongol Emperors, hard and despotic, paid little heed to the immediate needs of their people. Taking a long range view of the country's financial program, they did not deviate a hair's breadth from their policy of maintaining a paper currency, even though at times it was next to worthless. As each new emperor ascended the throne, he made adjustments and eradicated some of the evils. Never in a hurry, the methodical Chinese slowly adjusted themselves to the changing, but steadily improving, currency until the storied Kubla Khan took up the reins of government. At that time the Venetian adventurer and traveler, Marco Polo, arrived in China and did an excellent job of reporting Kubla Khan's establishment of an almost fantastic paper currency.

In the city of Cambaluc, now Peking, according to Marco Polo, the grand Khan set up a money mill from which was turned out an inexhaustible supply of paper currency. For paper he used the thin inner skin of mulberry bark, pounded to a pulp and rolled into sheets resembling black paper. When the sheets were ready for use, they were cut into oblong rectangles of different sizes and given the value of Venetian coins of varying denominations. The paper money was issued with as much pomp and ceremony as if it had been the purest gold. High government officials, in ceremonial regalia, affixed their signatures and seals to each note. A special emissary of the Great Khan stamped the notes in a bright vermilion with the royal seal.

With each batch of the money was issued a proclamation making counterfeiting punishable by death in the most violent form, and also making refusal to accept the notes in payment of bills a capital offense. The latter precaution seemed to be unnecessary since the notes were eagerly sought. Gold, silver, jewels, and wares of all kinds could readily be bought with them.

Caravans of merchants bearing gold, silver and precious stones journeyed to the Khan's palace where they exchanged their treasure for mulberry money. On those occasions the Khan summoned twelve men of broad experience to determine the value of the articles purchased. When the transaction was completed, the visiting merchants, their pouches bulging with the paper money, went through the bazaars of the city purchasing the merchandise they desired for use or for sale in their home communities.

As a further assurance of the value of the Khan's paper money, those holding worn or damaged notes could have them exchanged for new notes on payment of three per cent of their face value. Furthermore, those desiring gold or silver for commercial or manufacturing purposes could secure ingots of the precious metals on payment of paper money.

In spite of the precautions of the Khan, his currency eventually fell on evil days. The notes, while almost counterfeit-proof and highly acceptable, still had only the value of the paper on which they were printed, since they were not backed by either government gold or government silver. It is true that manufacturers and craftsmen could buy silver or gold from the royal hoard, but that was only through the generosity of the emperor who permitted a small part of his personal store of the precious metals to be diverted into channels of industry and art.

A counterfeit dollar bill, even if it be equal in artistry and workmanship to the point where it cannot be told from the genuine, is still worthless because it is not backed by a dollar's worth of collateral in the vaults of the Treasury. It is comparable to a check received from a person without funds or even an account in the bank on which it was drawn.

Our government now prints three kinds of paper money: Federal Reserve notes, silver certificates, and United States notes. Federal Reserve notes and United States notes are "convertible" only in that they are exchangeable for other types of legal money, of which silver dollars constitute one form. United States notes have no statutory metallic backing, and Federal Reserve notes may be secured in part by certain collateral. These notes are designed with exquisite artistry, and yet, in spite of their workmanship and the infinite care taken to make them counterfeit-proof, there exists in the United States a traffic, although a rapidly diminishing one, in counterfeit bills.

In many cases counterfeit rings operate like industrial or commercial concerns. They have their manufacturers, wholesalers and retailers, who make and deal in spurious bills as if they were soap or shoes. The retailer employs "shovers" who prowl the streets in search of victims. The shover can lay claim to practicing one of the very oldest professions, for in Biblical times we find the art of passing counterfeit money. The expression "shoving the queer" has been common in the underworld for centuries.

Unlike other major crimes, passing counterfeit money is done piecemeal, consequently a single offense is rarely considered worthy of being reported in the newspapers among the daily grist of crime.

Knowing little of the counterfeiter or his methods, I went to the United States Secret Service to get the facts. A division of the Treas-

You should know these faces.

WASHINGTON on all $1 bills.
JEFFERSON on all $2 bills.
LINCOLN on all $5 bills.
HAMILTON on all $10 bills.
JACKSON on all $20 bills.
GRANT on all $50 bills.

FRANKLIN on all $100 bills.

On less frequently used paper money, the portraits are:

McKINLEY on all $500 bills.
CLEVELAND on all $1,000 bills.
MADISON on all $5,000 bills.
CHASE on all $10,000 bills.

ury Department, the Secret Service is one of the oldest and most successful law enforcement agencies of the Federal Government. Established during the Civil War, it has been charged with the protection of the President of the United States, his family and the President-elect. The White House Police, a unit of the Secret Service, guards the Executive Mansion and its grounds.

It is also responsible for the suppression of counterfeiting and alteration of all paper money, coins, stamps, bonds, and sundry obligations of the United States and other governments.

It bears down with a heavy hand on counterfeiting, forging signatures, altering and fraudulent negotiation of United States Treasury checks and on other infractions of laws relating to the Treasury Department.

The Treasury Building, the Bureau of Engraving, and other buildings under the administration of the Treasury, including the gold depository at Fort Knox and the silver depository at West Point are protected by the Uniformed Force of the Secret Service.

Since I was concerned chiefly with getting information about money good and bad, I was delighted to learn that the Secret Service was at that moment engaged in a nation-wide campaign of education intended to make our entire population better informed about the money they handle daily. Police, peace officers, banks, schools, merchants, even street peddlers, were giving magnificent co-operation. In a short time millions of people, who had hitherto given the subject of counterfeiting little thought, became alert when handling coins and bills. Public school pupils became wary of plausible strangers who asked them to make purchases in stores and return the change from bills that were counterfeit. Merchants and their employees scrutinized the bills tendered them. Banks, railroad stations, hotels, theaters developed a consciousness for counterfeit almost over night.

A boy playing on the sidewalk saw a man leave a store with a small package which he promptly threw in an ash can, then went to another store across the street. Soon he appeared with another trifling purchase which he also threw away. The boy was mystified as he saw the stranger enter store after store, always getting rid of his purchase. Sensing that something was wrong, the lad told his father, who happened along, just what he had seen. Then father and son took up the stranger's trail and watched him as he went from store to store. Satisfied that the suspect was shoving counterfeit money, the boy's father reported what he had seen to a policeman, who, familiar with the methods of counterfeiters, knew that the shopper had a confederate in an automobile parked on a nearby street.

Presently the man who had been so closely watched turned into a side street, and went directly to a car in which another man was seated. Both were arrested, and in the car was found three thousand dollars' worth of counterfeit quarters.

A most ingenious preventive was developed and put in wide use by the Secret Service. It consists of a printed warning notice, bearing a ready reference that quickly enables the receiver of a counterfeit bill to detect it. The slip is pasted on the back of any show card advertising a popular brand of merchandise, or inconspicuously on the cash register. The card is then placed in a position that enables the clerk or cashier to refer to it without the knowledge of the "customer." So successful has been this innocent looking slip of paper that many counterfeiters have found themselves in jail as a result of it. Several large manufacturing concerns, on learning of the protection it gives their retailers, have embodied it in the millions of display cards they distribute to stores.

A typical case of how this paper sleuth works occurred recently. A good looking sedan pulled up to the curb outside a drugstore. One of the two men in it got out and after a quick look up and down the block entered the store. He was well-dressed and pleasant in manner. Purchasing a toothbrush in a most casual way, he gave the saleswoman a ten-dollar bill. The young woman went to the cash register to make change. She paused for a moment, resting her hand on the counter behind a card advertising a popular brand of cosmetics; then she rang up the sale on the register. As the drawer swung open she seemed embarrassed. "Sorry," she said, "I am a little short of change. If you will wait a moment, I will get it for you." The customer appeared impatient. Calling the proprietor the salesgirl said calmly, "I need change for this gentleman." The proprietor took the bill and went to the compounding department in the rear of the store as if he were going to the safe. Instead, he went to the telephone beside which was pasted one of the Secret Service refer-

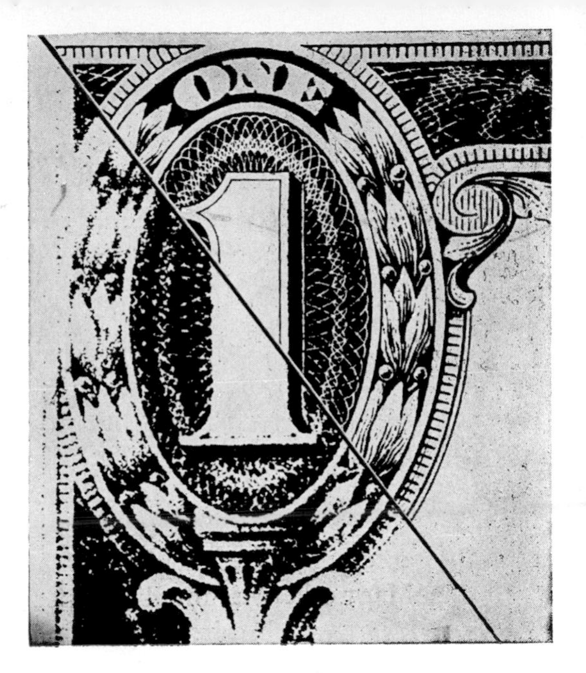

Above the dividing line, genuine. Below, counterfeit.

ence slips. Knowing that the salesgirl had change, he hastily compared the bill with the printed identifications and phoned the police. A radio alarm, giving the address of the drugstore and the nature of the offense, was broadcast from police headquarters. Two motorcycle policemen in the vicinity of the store sped to the scene. One pulled up beside the waiting car and arrested the occupant; the other entered the store and caught the counterfeiter. Before removing his prisoner, however, the policeman requested the salesgirl and the druggist to put their initials on the counterfeit note so that they could identify it in court.

An examination of the counterfeiter's car showed nothing out of the ordinary. In the glove compartment was an electric flashlight. On finding it the policeman smiled grimly. "The same old trick," he said as he unscrewed the cap and drew from the battery compartment a fat roll of counterfeit bills.

Speaking of the reference slip recently, a notorious counterfeiter in Kansas City said, "That measly bit of paper has spoiled the racket."

And so it has. For while arrests have increased, counterfeit note cases have decreased as much as ninety-seven per cent. Once, in an interview, Frank J. Wilson, former Chief of the United States Secret Service, said, "An ounce of crime prevention is worth five pounds of crime cure."

Over a five-year period prior to the inauguration of the Secret Service Crime Prevention program, the losses from counterfeit money averaged more than one million dollars a year, while the expenses of investigation, prosecution and jailing of counterfeiters cost another million or more a year. During that period, the public aided the counterfeiters materially by a complete carelessness in accepting money without a thought of whether it was good or bad. Many otherwise intelligent people who had never come into personal contact with crime, upon finding themselves victims of one of the meanest crimes on the calendar, pocketed their loss without so much as reporting it to the proper authorities. These good people helped victimize their communities as completely as if they had accompanied the counterfeiter on his daily rounds. They seemed to forget that the shover, in order to make his trade profitable, must gather in many victims. He leaves a trail behind him as broad as the Lincoln Highway. Nearly every victim has a good description of him, a valuable aid to the police when they go on the hunt for him.

A typical case of this carelessness came to my attention recently while talking with a shopkeeper in a community of about twelve thousand. Shortly before closing time, a well-dressed man entered his store and made a two-dollar purchase, for which he tendered a new twenty-dollar bill. The merchant did not have sufficient change. "How much have you got?" asked the stranger. The merchant replied that he had seventeen dollars. "That's all right," said the customer, "I'll take this," pointing to a dollar article. The gullible merchant wrapped up the purchase and handed over seventeen dollars change to the stranger, even thanking him for being so considerate. The following day the shopkeeper went to his bank to make a cash deposit that included the twenty-dollar bill he had received the evening before. As the teller deftly counted the bills, he stopped abruptly and closely examined one of them which was new and crisp. "This is a counterfeit," he said. The merchant was shocked. "It can't be," he said. "That was given to me by a customer, a very decent man." "Do you know him well?" asked the teller. "Frankly, no," replied the merchant. "He was a stranger but a fine looking gentleman." The teller smiled, "I know all about him," he said. "You are the third victim I have met this morning."

Of twenty-eight householders and their families whom I interviewed lately, only two knew the characteristics of the bills they handle every day. One of the two acquired his knowledge from literature published by the Secret Service in its "Know your Money" campaign against counterfeiting. Not one of the group had ever examined a bill under a magnifying glass and none was conscious of the exquisite workmanship which is our chief protection against the counterfeiters.

Every bill, whether its denomination is one dollar or one thousand dollars, is an almost perfect impression of the plate from which it was printed. No matter how skilled the counterfeiter may be, he cannot make a perfect replica of that plate. To do so, he must have the original which is safely guarded in the government vaults. In lieu of the original plate, therefore, he works from a bill of the denomination he wishes to counterfeit. He begins by photographing it and transferring the image to metal. During each step, he loses some of the clear-cut sharpness of the original. Those who have dabbled in photography know that a copy is never as sharp or as clear as the original. The plate he makes is, therefore, inferior to the original by a wide margin. The paper he uses is not only inferior, but of a different composition since all genuine money paper is made from a formula controlled and guarded by the government. His ink is also a different formula from that used by the government printers, which is not available to the public. His printing press is usually a run-of-the-mill commercial affair, incapable of doing the faultless work demanded of the superb government presses. With all these handicaps, it is not surprising that "bad money" is bad on every count, including its appearance.

The counterfeit bill *always* lacks the crisp sharpness of the genuine. The individual lines so meticulously executed by the government engraver are uncertain and broken in the work of the criminal money-maker, particularly where they fade into a high light.

The counterfeiter's greatest bugaboo is the portrait that appears

on every bill. These portraits are intended to make the identification of bills of any denomination more certain and more easy. Regardless of the type, all bills of the same denomination bear the same portrait as follows:

WASHINGTON	on $1 bills.	JACKSON	on $20 bills.
JEFFERSON	on $2 bills.	GRANT	on $50 bills.
LINCOLN	on $5 bills.	FRANKLIN	on $100 bills.
HAMILTON	on $10 bills.		

Other paper money issued by the United States bears portraits of:

McKINLEY	on $500 bills.	MADISON	on $5,000 bills.
CLEVELAND	on $1,000 bills.	CHASE	on $10,000 bills.

The man who made this counterfeit bill is now in Leavenworth Penitentiary. When compared with a genuine bill the portrait is flat and spotty, the background around the head is smudged and dark. The fine lines of the border are not distinct. The numbers and seal are crudely printed. On all genuine bills the printing must *be perfect.*

The defects in the counterfeiting process mar the likeness of the portrait on the spurious bill; the delicate shadings that make the head on the genuine bill so lifelike are lost in reproduction; the shadows are heavy and the highlights are chalky. Parts of the portrait merge into the smudgy background. If examined under a glass, the background behind the portrait on a good bill is composed of sharp cross-lines between which the white paper shows, as through the meshes of a net. The eyes of a portrait in a genuine bill are executed in amazingly sensitive lines that give the whole face life and expression. In the "phony" bill the lines that make up the eye are broken and blurred, giving the whole face a staring or startled expression.

Look at the colored Treasury seal on a good bill. The saw-tooth points around the rim are sharp and even; in the counterfeit they are usually uneven and broken. The serial number on a bill should be firm and evenly printed; on a counterfeit the digits are uneven, often with broken lines and badly spaced. The paper on which a genuine bill is printed is easily distinguishable as a result of the tiny fibers in its texture. Counterfeiters sometimes imitate the red and blue threads with colored inks.

There is an erroneous idea that if a genuine bill is rubbed on paper, the ink will not come off. The ink can be rubbed from bad and good bills alike. If in doubt about the genuineness of a bill, the owner should go to a bank and get expert advice before offering it as legal tender. In case the bill is counterfeit, the transaction may cause serious trouble for the person "passing" it.

A much practiced trick of the counterfeiter is the manipulation of two good bills, say of ten-dollar and one-dollar denominations in such a way that they can be passed as two good ten-dollar bills. This ruse can always be detected by observing the face of every bill received. A ten-dollar bill with the portrait of Washington on it is spurious just as a one-dollar bill with the face of Jefferson on it is worthless. Although practiced by counterfeiters, this is not true counterfeiting, since no plates or printing are involved. It is rather criminal mutilation of currency, for which there is a heavy penalty.

Bills worn almost beyond recognition or accidentally mutilated or charred may be sent in to be redeemed by the Treasury. A staff of employees specialize in inspecting money for redemption. So expert are these men that the Treasury often gives new money for bills that to the untrained eye are beyond recognition.

The wear and tear on paper money is very great. Every day millions of dollars' worth come in from the banks to the Treasury to be destroyed by burning. In a single month bills with a face value of nearly three hundred million dollars have been sent to the incinerators to be burned under the watchful eyes of Treasury officials.

It should be remembered that counterfeit money is deliberately passed by strangers. Occasionally, a person known to be of good character offers a counterfeit bill without knowledge of its worthlessness. In either case, action should be taken at once. In the event

Counterfeiters caught in the act.

Arrest of "shover." *Arrest of accomplice leaving get-away car.*

of a stranger, the police should be notified without delay, while the person who innocently tenders a bad bill should be instructed to report it either to the nearest Secret Service office, the local police or the local bank giving, if possible, a description of the passer and other particulars of the transaction in which the bill was received. The person who accepts a counterfeit is the loser. There is no redress either from the government or the bank.

I am informed by the Secret Service that boys and girls of school age are often used as innocent accomplices by counterfeiters. A stranger, man or woman, pulls up to the curb in an automobile that may be a jaloppy or a brand new car and cheerfully calls to a youngster passing by. "Say, son, do me a favor?" The boy sees that the stranger is well dressed and nicely spoken. "Sure," he replies. Then the stranger hands him a bill saying, "Hop into that drugstore and get me a package of cigarettes. I don't like to leave this car here alone." The boy hurries to do the errand and soon returns with the purchase and change. He notices that the stranger looks shiftily around as he grabs the package and the money. Then without even a "thank you" the car is shot away from the curb and is soon lost in the traffic.

The boy, a little bewildered, wonders why the polite stranger should suddenly act so churlishly. He finds out later when he reaches home. The druggist has telephoned his mother that her boy gave him a counterfeit ten-dollar bill when purchasing cigarettes and asks her to send over a good bill immediately. The mother questions her son and learns about the stranger for whom he did the errand. A sensible woman, she reports the case to the police. The boy has been taught to be wary of pleasant strangers.

Although I have attended many police line-ups, I am still astonished at the parade of "nice looking" people who prove to be out-and-out rascals. A Secret Service man said to me recently, "Remember, not all strangers are counterfeiters, but all counterfeiters are strangers."

One of the most slippery of criminals, the counterfeiter is rarely caught red-handed, yet the Secret Service annually convicts about ninety-seven per cent of those arrested. The perpetual alertness of this magnificent law enforcement agency, combined with the almost superhuman care with which the United States Bureau of Engraving and Printing prepares our vast paper currency, are responsible for the sometimes insurmountable obstacles in the path of the counterfeiters. It is safe to say that if either or both of these organizations were to relax their vigilance, the United States would be flooded with worthless money within a year.

The Bureau of Engraving and Printing is one of the world's industrial wonders. It is a huge manufacturing plant in which the product, running into billions of units, maintains a standard of microscopic perfection such as has never been equaled in any line. Its men, materials, and machines must be the best the world affords or it would fail in its purpose. Its more than seven thousand eight hundred employees are hand-picked, not only for their skill, but for their personal integrity. They know to the last man and woman that there are no such words as "fair" or "passable" or "pretty good" in the vocabulary of their job. Only indisputable perfection in every step and every process will satisfy.

When a new note is to be issued, a conference of officials is called, and the character of the design is discussed. The rough ideas are given to a designer from the Engraving Division with instructions to embody them in a comprehensive sketch or "model." When the sketch is ready, the officials sit in conference again and discuss it at length, criticizing here, suggesting there, until all are agreed on every detail.

Alterations and corrections are made by the designer, after which the sketch is submitted to the Secretary of the Treasury for final approval. The design sketch is now reproduced in soft steel by engravers, each of whom specializes in a certain part of the work. One man engraves the portrait, another does the lettering, still another does the ornamentation, and so on.

The engravers work with a steel tool which has a diamond-shaped point capable of cutting a perfectly clean line. The work, done under a powerful enlarging glass, is a constant strain on the nerves of the engraver; the slightest slip of the tool or miscalculation of width or depth of line destroys weeks or months of labor. When finished, the plate on which the engravers have worked is called a "die." Its soft steel is hardened by being heated in cyanide of sodium and instantly dipped into a brine or oil bath. The plate is now ready for the transfer press in which a cylinder of soft steel is rolled over its hardened surface under tremendous pressure. The soft steel of the cylinder or roll is pressed into the engraved lines of the die, much as you might press putty on a coin. A perfect impression in which the engraved or sunken lines of the die become raised lines on the roll. The metal of the cylinder is now hardened by the same process as was used to harden the die. The roll is now made to force an impression into a steel plate in which the lines are cut just as they were in the original die. When this plate is hardened and cleaned, it is ready for the printer.

The reason for this apparently roundabout process is a good one. The original die, so laboriously engraved line by line, is valuable beyond price. If used for printing, it would eventually wear out and become useless. Therefore, it is held as a master plate from which many rolls can be made and from these, in turn, any number of plates to be used on several presses.

Another method of making plates, known as the electrolytic

process, is also used by the Bureau. Through this process, the life of the valuable original plate has been greatly lengthened. The hand-engraved plate is placed in an electrolytic bath where microscopic particles of metal are deposited all over its surface, and allowed to build up until they have reached a certain depth or thickness. This deposit, now solid metal, is called an "alto." The face of the alto which was in contact with the plate is a perfect impression of the original. The alto is now placed in the bath to undergo the same building-up process as the original plate. The metal deposited on it consists of a layer of nickel backed up by electrolytic iron which, when removed from the alto, carries an exact reproduction of the original design. This plate is called a "basso" and is used in the actual printing. This basso, or printing plate, is given a final coating of wear-resisting chromium three ten-thousandths of an inch in thickness. Since there is no pressure or wear, the alto can be used to make any number of plates.

Dies, rolls, plates, altos and negatives are placed in the burglar-proof plate vault each evening, and are kept under heavy guard. They may be taken from the vault only on properly signed requisitions.

One of the earliest safeguards to the notes and securities of the government was adopted during the Civil War, when a distinctive paper, to be used exclusively for the government, was adopted.

In 1885 a new paper, finished on both sides and having a silk fiber embedded in it, was put in use. Cotton fibers are used today. At the paper factory in which it is made, the work is done under the direct supervision of an agent appointed by the Secretary of the Treasury and responsible to him. Every sheet made must be accounted for.

The paper used in our bank notes has been a serious stumbling block to the counterfeiters. They have never been able to make even a good imitation of it, due to the secret processes used in its manufacture.

The inks used in printing paper money are made from secret formulae in laboratories within the Bureau. Like the paper, the ink must be unchanging in quality and characteristics. So closely is it guarded, there is a collection made of all waste ink at the close of each day. This is returned to the Ink Making Division, where it is reconditioned and stored for further use.

Reeding on edge of genuine half-dollar on top and counterfeit on bottom.

The first step in the printing operation is the withdrawal from the Division of Paper Custody the paper required. This is done on requisition by the Wetting Division. The paper is received in sealed packages of one thousand sheets. The packages are counted, the seals are broken, the paper is weighed and taken to operatives who count the number of sheets in each package and sign the attached tags to signify the correctness of the count.

The paper is now ready to be wet, preparatory to printing. Moist paper is more pliable, and the engravings can be printed with less pressure and with a clearer impression than on dry paper.

The wetting is done by machines on which the sheets are automatically fed to a felt blanket under a stream of water. After running through a set of rolls which regulate the amount of moisture in the paper, the sheets are counted and stacked in lots of one hundred, then moved to the stock room and weighed. Here the bundles are wrapped in moist cloths and placed under heavy weights. After three or four days, the moisture has seeped into every fiber of the paper.

Through each step of the wetting process, the packages of paper are tagged by the person handling them. The tags record the contents of each package, the class and denomination of the work for which it is intended, also the name of the handler, so that if an error should be detected the person responsible for it can be traced and the error rectified.

Each printer's assistant draws paper for the day's work, presenting a draw slip on which are stated the amount, class, and denomination of the paper required. The paper is counted again at the press and the printer gives the Wetting Section a receipt for it. Should an error be found, it must be investigated and rectified before the printing begins.

Each printing press is operated by a printer and two assistants. Each press has four plates. When the press is put in motion by the printer, each plate in turn passes under a lightly inked roller which presses the ink into its delicately engraved lines. The excess ink on the surface is removed by a mechanical "wiper," that is, all but a thin film which is removed by the hand of the printer. This hand operation also polishes the surface of the plate without disturbing the ink deposited in the thousands of minute lines. The assistant, who sits at the front of the press, registers a sheet of paper accurately on the plate just as it approaches the impression roller which presses the paper down on the ink-filled lines. As the plate comes from the roller, a second assistant lifts the sheet from the plate, examines it carefully and sets it on the pile, printed side up. Tissue paper is then placed over the newly printed sheet to prevent the fresh ink from offsetting on to the next sheet which is placed, printed side down, on the tissue. This arrangement of sheets is alternated through the run. If the impression is too light or too heavy, the second assistant notifies the printer who immediately adjusts the press.

Each time two hundred sheets are printed throughout the day, a messenger collects them and takes them to the Examining Division, where they are counted and placed in drying boxes.

When quitting time comes around, the printer carefully washes all ink from the plates, and locks them securely to the press under a steel cover. However, before this is done, there begins a system of checking and re-checking. Representatives of the Wetting Section, Examining Division, and of the Custodian of Presses who is in charge of the counting registers on the presses, get together and check each printer's work as to class, denomination and the number of sheets printed. The records of all three must agree before anyone is allowed to leave the building.

The newly printed sheets are placed in heated rooms known

The four common tests for a counterfeit coin:

A. It feels "greasy."

B. It is soft to the blade of a knife.

C. It has a dull sound when dropped on a hard surface.

D. It turns black if acid is dropped on it.

as drying boxes, where they remain overnight. The next morning the tissues between the sheets are removed, and the sheets are sent to the examiners who count them and examine them for imperfections. The perfect work is made up into packages of one thousand sheets; paper straps indicating hundreds are inserted. Each printer's work, perfect and imperfect, is carefully recorded. The imperfect sheets are destroyed; the perfect are taken to the vaults. So far, only one side of the note is printed. When the other side is printed, the whole procedure is repeated—checking and re-checking, counting and re-counting.

When the printing is completed, the sheets are again placed in the heavily guarded vault, from where the notes are sent to the sizing room. Here each sheet is coated with a mixture of thin glue and alum, after which it is thoroughly dried. Again the sheets are counted and checked and arranged in even piles.

The sizing gives a better finish to the currency, strengthening the paper, making it more resistant to dirt, grease and wear and, thereby, lengthening the life of the note.

The money is still by no means finished. It is now put through what is known as a platering operation. The sheets are placed between heavy cardboards, seventy to a pile. Sheets of steel are placed on the top, on the bottom, and in the center of the pile which is known as a "form." The form is run through a plater press under a pressure of five thousand pounds to the square inch. This pressure has the same effect on the sheets as a tailor's steam press has on wrinkled trousers. They come through smooth, flat, and well groomed.

Here again they are counted and checked against the records before being placed in the vaults where they remain until they are ready for trimming. This is done by a machine that slices off the edges of the sheets so that all margins are equal. Again they are counted and checked with the records and returned to the vaults in packages of one thousand sheets with twelve notes to a sheet.

So far, the notes have little more value than so many sheets of printed paper. The many precautions taken are intended to check errors rather than to prevent theft.

In the Numbering Section, to which they are taken next, the sheets are converted into negotiable money. Here extra safety precautions are taken; the work is done in wire cages and armed guards are placed to see that no employee enters or leaves without proper permission.

Before the final operations are begun, the sheets are again counted and checked. The presses used here are specially designed for the work. Mechanical feeders send the sheets through the presses. In their passage through these complex machines, the number and seal are printed on the face of each note. Each sheet is cut into the required number of notes which are then counted and gathered into bundles of one hundred. The notes are then carefully examined and counted by expert operators who check the number of each bill to determine its correctness. The notes are now made up into packages which are secured by electrically welded steel bands. They are then wrapped in heavy paper and securely closed with government paper seals.

At the end of the day each note and package handled in the Numbering Section must be accounted for. This brief summary of how our money is made shows clearly the futility of counterfeiting, at least on a scale large enough to threaten the integrity of our paper money.

To know your money, study this diagram. It illustrates the position and character of important currency features.

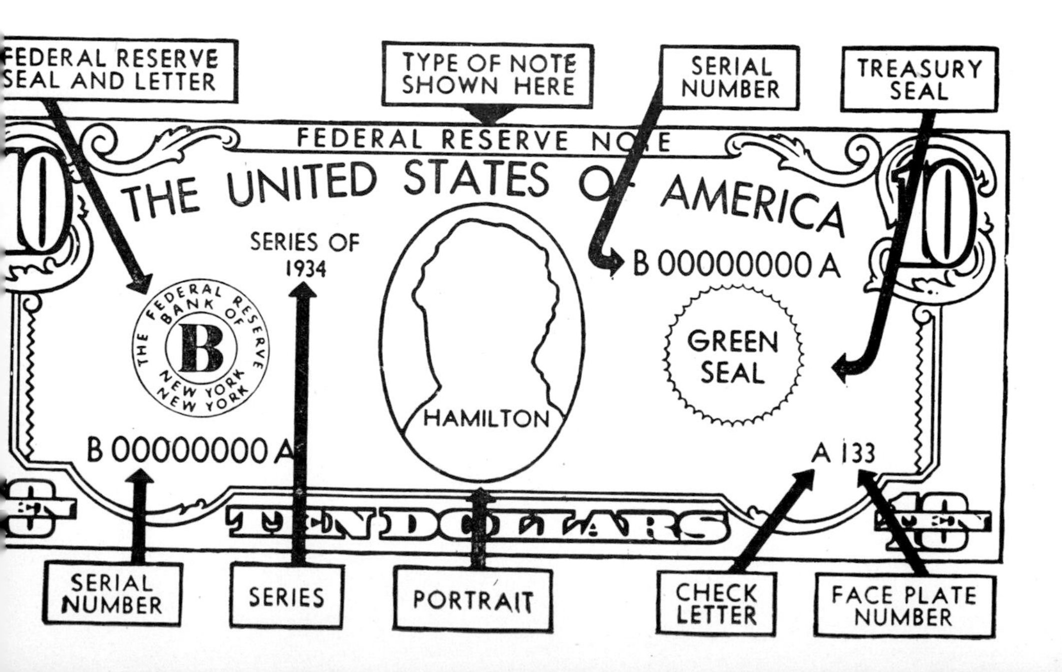

Fort Knox, the world's greatest treasure house. Billions of dollars' worth of gold is stored here and safeguarded by heavily armed guards every second of the day and night.

7

When the Treasury Department was established by the first Congress, and for several years thereafter, Philadelphia was the temporary capital of the nation. Meanwhile a scheme of more or less co-ordinated buildings to house the government in the District of Columbia was formulated. Included in the project were plans for a small wooden building to shelter the Treasury Department. It was designed by an English architect, George Hatfield, and was built on the corner of Pennsylvania Avenue and Fifteenth Street. The tiny Treasury building was opened for business in 1800 when the new City of Washington became the seat of the Federal Government. Within a year it was almost destroyed by fire, but it was repaired and continued in use until 1814 when it was burned down by British soldiers. Its records and documents were consumed. Another building was erected but that, too, went up in flames seven years later. At last Congress decided to build a structure of stone and mortar that would at least reduce the fire hazard. Then began a

TREASURE HOUSE

period of interminable haggling in which the location, plans, and materials were condemned and defended. President Andrew Jackson, impatient to get the work done and over with, pleaded with both sides without result.

Early one morning while the members of the carping committees were still abed, the President, accompanied by a small group of determined men, quietly left the Executive mansion and strode across lots to the vacant site of the Treasury. They paced off distances, surveyed the grades and consulted now and then.

While walking across the site, President Jackson stopped abruptly and threw a keen glance around the area. Then planting his gold-headed walking-stick in the soft earth said, "Right here is where I want the cornerstone." And right there the cornerstone of the United States Treasury stands to this day.

Soon from its scraggly surroundings a building of classic design began to rise in spite of political squabbling. The original design was not followed faithfully. The architect's plans called for an expenditure of one million five hundred thousand dollars; this was pared down to less than seven hundred thousand dollars. The result was inevitable. Within a few years the Treasury Department had outgrown its building. Addition after addition was built, none of them adequate. In about thirty years, additions to the original structure cost nearly six million dollars. Later changes brought the total to about eight million dollars.

When the building was opened, candles were used for illumination and open fireplaces supplied the heat. One of the original fireplaces is still being used in the office of the Secretary of the Treasury. This delightful room, in which many generations of Secretaries have worked, is, in its beautiful simplicity and quiet furnishings, a haven of peace in the administrative turmoil seething for miles around it.

One morning recently I arrived at the Secretary's office by appointment and was escorted to an anteroom in which a military aide and a secretary kept watchful eyes on the arrival and departure of visitors. A group of Treasury officials had just completed a conference with the Secretary and were leaving. After announcing me, the military aide, a Lieutenant Commander, ushered me into the historic chamber.

This remarkable machine prints the number and colored seal that appear on bills of every denomination.

From high in the branches of a sun-dappled maple outside, the twittering notes of a song sparrow came through the broad open windows. Somehow they brightened up the silent interior, the walls of which were hung with life-size portraits of Secretaries who had gone to their fathers long since.

A little beyond the center of the room stood a large unadorned desk; on its broad top there was not as much as a scrap of paper. Behind it sat the Secretary of the Treasury looking, I thought, a little weary but alert and vital. His deep baritone voice was kindly, in fact, gentle. His speech was deliberate rather than slow. His long slightly pallid face was lighted by the most brilliant pair of eyes I had ever seen. They sparkled and scintillated, yet were as steady and penetrating as those of an eagle. His shapely hands were sensitive, but composed. When he spoke, the Secretary's words were few and well-chosen. Like most men of his caliber, he is a listener rather than a talker. There was not even a touch of formality in the interview. It was a friendly chat, such as one might enjoy at a club or the home of a friend. Nowhere in the Secretary's suite was there hurry or bustle. There seemed to be the leisurely tempo of a well-ordered house.

It was difficult for me to realize that across the desk beside which I sat and from the quiet man in front of me came edicts daily that caused the heads of nations to sit up and listen.

When I left the ancient building, I carried away with me a strange picture of the Treasury Department and its functions. Considering money as the blood stream of our nation, I saw the Treasury as a gigantic heart throbbing ceaselessly, keeping the life-giving money tide in perpetual circulation. Through a complex venous system that branches out into the sources of revenue, a stream of money is pumped into the Treasury heart only to be pumped out again through an arterial system that carries the money stream to one hundred and thirty million destinations—the American people.

The money veins draw their stream from income and other taxes, duties on imports, miscellaneous internal revenues, and collections of fees, fines, penalties, forfeitures, sales of government properties, and a score of other sources. The money arteries form a veritable network of conduits through which the money stream passes out into the body economic. There are in fact some eight thousand of them, since that is the number of appropriation accounts on the Treasury's books.

This great circulatory system and its hundreds of ramifications are under the control of the Secretary of the Treasury. He is assisted by three Assistant Secretaries who are appointed by the President, and a Fiscal Assistant Secretary who is appointed by the Secretary of the Treasury in accordance with civil service laws.

The duties first assigned to the Treasury Department were to collect taxes and other revenues, to borrow money when necessary, to keep the national funds safely, and to pay the government bills under orders of the Congress. Those are still its chief functions. Among its more recently acquired responsibilities are coining money and regulating its value.

When President Washington appointed his aide-de-camp, Alexander Hamilton, as the first Secretary of the Treasury, about one hundred persons were employed in the tiny Treasury building. This force was gradually supplemented by collectors of customs and collectors of internal revenue.

In those early days smuggling was practiced or encouraged by rich and poor alike with a consequent depletion of the national revenue. Much of the contraband came from foreign ports and entered the United States by way of isolated coves and backwaters along the coast. To prevent this loss of revenue, Hamilton was authorized by President Washington according to an act of Congress to organize the Revenue Cutter service, which is today the United States Coast Guard.

During the Civil War, the Treasury was given the task of providing paper currency, then called "greenbacks." The subsequent wave of counterfeiting made necessary the organization of the United States Secret Service.

All moneys entering or leaving the Treasury go through the office of the Treasurer of the United States, who must not be confused with the Secretary of the Treasury. The Treasurer is the official custodian of the nation's money. He receives it from the various agencies that collect revenue whether in the form of customs, taxes, loans or any of the other revenue activities, and it is he who pays it out. In addition all new paper currency is delivered to him by the Bureau of Engraving and Printing. He redeems the daily flood of paper money unfit for further circulation and issues the Daily Statement of the Treasury which tells the state of the country's money affairs.

The Comptroller of the Currency is the connecting link between the Treasury and the nation's banks. It is he who charters and supervises the national banks and grants them permission to establish branches. Should any of those banks become insolvent, the Comptroller appoints receivers to liquidate their assets and distribute the proceeds to the creditors. He makes an annual report to

Congress and recommends such changes in the banking laws as he considers necessary.

During several visits to the Treasury Department, I was deeply impressed by the extreme contrasts in the attitude of the workers toward the great flood of money that daily flows in and out of our national treasure house. Here men handle billions of dollars as if they were dealing in beans, and yet the thought of the discrepancy of a dollar in the Treasury's accounts would throw them into a cold sweat.

One afternoon while flying from Washington to New York after one of those visits, it occurred to me that few of us had a full appreciation of what a billion really means. In an effort to get a grasp of the magnitude of a billion, I thought of it in terms of minutes rather than dollars. The plane was hurtling through a

As the sheets of currency come from the presses of the Bureau of Engraving and Printing, they are carefully scrutinized by hundreds of examiners for the slightest imperfection.

fog that shut out the wonderful panorama that lay below us. To pass the time, I began to calculate the number of minutes that had elapsed during the nineteen centuries since the birth of Christ. To my amazement I discovered that only a billion minutes had ticked by between that holy night at Bethlehem and the Christmas of 1904.

In the language of today's economy the word "billion" is used with startling frequency and bewildering implications. We read of appropriations and expenditures involving hundreds of billions of dollars. These astronomical sums long since have passed the total of all our monetary wealth; in short, we have appropriated or spent more money than we own. To the lay mind, that means we are insolvent or in plain language "dead broke." We are far from it, however. As a matter of fact, instead of being poorer as the result of our huge spending, we are richer, vastly richer, financially, physically, spiritually.

The vast sums going out of the U.S. Treasury to pay our bills are not *spent;* they are merely dispersed into our own national industry and commerce. They are, in fact, pumped with rapid heartbeats into the arteries that carry them back to the American people in the form of wages, salaries, commissions, and dividends.

I attended the launching of a large naval vessel recently. The Brooklyn Navy Yard, where she was built, had for a short hour a holiday air. Thousands of invited guests filled every vantage point in the vicinity of the magnificent ship. A Navy band made the air tingle with lively tunes. One of the world's greatest financiers, who stood beside me, was as jittery with excitement as a boy at a circus.

As the vessel slid down the smoking ways, someone near by remarked, "There goes fifty million dollars we can kiss good-by!" I was startled for a moment; there was something eerie in his words. It was as if I had seen a man walk to the gallows. When I stopped to reason it out, as I did later, I became aware of something that had never occurred to me before. The fifty million dollars the government had spent on the battleship had been paid to American laborers, artisans, technicians, engineers, manufacturers, and stockholders. Her thousands of tons of steel had come from American steel mills employing thousands of Americans. Her mighty engines were the product of American engineering and mechanical skill. Her guns, torpedoes, and ammunition were fashioned by American hands. The thousand electric motors installed within her were American as Plymouth Rock. The raw materials represented in her great hulk were mined, or felled, or pumped by Americans from the great national wealth of America. Every state in the Union contributed to the vast pile of materials from which she was made. Thousands of American banks profited directly or indirectly from the expenditure of the fifty millions she cost.

Later when she was commissioned and put out to sea, she became an American community in which one thousand two hundred hand-picked Americans lived, and ate, and slept, and pursued their daily occupations as if their ship had been a town in the heart of the state after which she was named. The men of this floating community were clothed and fed and cared for, physically and morally, according to standards impossible to attain in civilian life. In her cold storage hung prime beef, lamb, pork and vegetable food, mountains of it, raised in a score of states. Flour from American wheat, canned goods from American factories, clothing of a dozen kinds including shoes, blankets, and storm-coats; in fact, every commodity of comfortable living made in hundreds of factories all over the country were piled in hold and lazarette and paid for on the barrel head in good American money worth a hundred cents on the dollar. This is the money that seeped in greater or lesser quantities into millions of American homes in some form of income. And from this income the recipients took a proportionate share, and sent it back through the financial veins to the country's financial heart, the Treasury, in the form of war bonds, income tax and other levies. Never was finer illustration of the conversion through work of our natural wealth into money in the pockets of the people.

"But what of the expendibles, the things destroyed in the process of war?" one may ask. "Aren't they a total loss?"

The answer is, "No." Take a torpedo, perhaps the most expendible of major weapons. Its use, successful or unsuccessful, means its loss. If it finds its mark, it has fulfilled its purpose by destroying enemy property; if it misses, which it does with regrettable frequency, it sinks forever into the cold silence of the sea. In either case its physical loss in value is but a few hundred pounds of metal and chemicals. There is no actual financial loss to the country. Its cost to the government was, let us say, twelve thousand dollars. That cost represents actual money paid to the builders of the torpedo who, in turn, pass it along to the management, the labor groups, the stockholders of the company, and to the other manufacturers who supplied component parts reserving, of course, a share for surplus, income tax and government bonds.

Broadly speaking, the more of the twelve thousand dollars the draftsman, the machinist, the truck driver or the president of the company receives, the more he returns to the government in the form of income tax. But that is not all. He contributes a little here and a little there in taxes on certain commodities. Every time he puts gas in his automobile, he pays a few cents tax on every gallon. When he buys packaged articles to which are affixed the little blue stamp, he contributes a few cents to the internal revenue. If he purchases an article that was made in another country, he puts up his share of the duty that was paid by the importer. These trifling amounts that we all contribute daily to the government mount up to hundreds of millions of dollars annually.

All these taxes, and duties, and other sources of fixed contributions to the government fall far below the amount required to run the country, particularly in time of war. Then the government goes out like any other well-ordered business and borrows the amount it requires, putting up gilt-edge security in the form of bonds and paying interest on every dollar it borrows. In doing this, it performs two important functions; it secures the necessary funds to carry on its projects, and it sets up a preventive mechanism against inflation by drawing off excess money at a time when commodities are scarce, and when people are tempted to outbid each other for the things they *think* they require.

As the money is pumped into the Treasury from all these sources, it is pumped out again in millions or billions and into the pockets of the people who again send back their quotas to the government. And so it goes, year in and year out. The nation's money flows from people to government and from government to people in a perpetual Money-Go-Round.

As this is written, our government's expenditures have exceeded its income by some 9 billion dollars, thus leaving the national budget unbalanced and thrifty citizens disturbed. Because of our enormous resources, however, the fiscal outlook is far from dangerously serious.

One may well ask here, "From where will all this money come?" The answer is simple. It will come from the mines, the forests, the wheat fields and our other natural resources, through the labor of our people. From there and no place else can it come, for money is only a token of labor performed.

Then one may ask further, "How great is our natural wealth from which these billions must come?"

The Secretary of the Interior, who is entrusted with our natural wealth, as the Secretary of the Treasury is entrusted with our money wealth, recently answered this by listing the assets of the United States.

In dollars and cents, coal is our biggest physical asset. We have nearly ten *trillion* dollars' worth waiting to be mined and converted into money. Such a quantity of any commodity cannot be comprehended except by the mind of the scientist. The late Charles Steinmetz, a leader in the world of science and a wizard in mathematics, once estimated that from a single year's output of our coal mines, a wall thirty feet in height and ten feet in thickness could be built around the United States. Some estimate that we have enough coal in our subterranean bins to last us five thousand years.

We have a buried stock pile of iron ore valued at sixteen billions of dollars, enough to last us fifty years at normal consumption. Iron, even now, is being replaced by lighter metals and in some cases plastics, so that we may never need to scrape the bottom of the pile.

Our underground reservoir of petroleum and natural gas is appraised at the tidy sum of seventy-five billion dollars, enough heat and power for generations to come.

The water power of the United States has been valued at five billion dollars by the Secretary of the Interior. This "white coal," as someone has called it, generates about twenty million horsepower a year. It would require thirty million tons of mined coal to furnish the same power.

Then there are our forests, and farms, and fisheries with a valuation of sixty-five billions.

To round out our list of assets, the Secretary includes our manufacturing plants, and public and private utilities, and sets a value on them of one hundred thirteen billion dollars. He gives our public and private buildings a valuation of one hundred forty billions.

A summary of the above shows that our physical assets amount to twelve thousand billion dollars, while our public debt may mount to as high as three hundred billion. In other words we are, broadly speaking, in the position of a merchant who owed three hundred dollars but who had a stock of twelve thousand dollars' worth of merchandise on hand, ready to be sold over the counter and converted into cash, a task that would call for long hours and hard work.

Our twelve trillion dollar assets tell but part of the story for over and above that mighty mountain of wealth, we have that great-

Millions of dollars in paper money that has outlived its usefulness is burned in this incinerating furnace under the watchful eyes of Treasury officials.

est of all assets—the inventive genius, the enterprise and the energy of one hundred thirty million free people. There are still untold riches to be taken from the air and from the sea. Nitrogen, magnesium, and bromine are but a few of them. A vast project of scientific research lies before us. Chemistry, metallurgy, electronics, agricultural biology, plastics, and a hundred of the other sciences offer fields in which the laboratory will sow the seeds and industry will do the harvesting.

From coast to coast, and from border to border our country is sprinkled with thousands of new factories, the finest in equipment and personnel the world has ever seen. They are unburdened by heavy debt, the American people have seen to that. In short we approach a new era, girded for battle against the dark horsemen of the Apocalypse that have ridden roughshod over all peoples since the world began.

When George Washington organized the United States Treasury, the country with a population of less than four million was practically without funds. Whatever small reserves the colonies possessed had been depleted to extinction by a hard-fought war. Such continental currency as had been issued from time to time soon lost its value. With the exception of the commonwealth of Massachusetts, ventures in coining by the individual colonies invariably ended in disaster, so that when Secretary of the Treasury Hamilton took office, he had a scanty store of money to administer. But neither he, nor Washington, nor Jefferson, nor the other founders of the Republic were trammeled by doubt as to the ultimate prosperity of the newly born nation. They knew that to the west, to the north, and to the south lay fabulous wealth, waiting for the ax and plow and miners' drill, waiting for the labor, not of the four millions, but of the generations to come. They knew well the process of converting the natural wealth into money by the admixture of enterprise and sweat. In their foresight they saw the pitiful little issue of silver money made from Washington's tableware grow into the billions that flow daily into and out of the Treasury of our time.

The most valuable commodity the young country possessed was the inspired labor of its people, whether they built roads or ships, dug potatoes or iron ore. The plow, the fishing net, and the ever-ready musket requisitioned from the earth, the forest, and the sea the ample store of simple food that built strong men and women who toiled from dawn till dark building for the generations to come. None was very rich and none was very poor. There was neither Capital nor Labor as we understand them today, for every man was a capitalist and every man a laborer. Then, as now, capital provided the tools with which labor fashioned into money the natural wealth provided by the Almighty for both of them. It was not the hours that men labored but rather the result of their labors that made us the richest country in the world.

Again as the result of the prodigious waste of war, we find ourselves heavily burdened with debt, a debt which America will pay even to its last creditor. That our obligations are the heaviest in history is obvious, but our resources are the greatest the world has ever known.

It must be remembered that our lands bursting with wealth, our factories pulsing with mechanical marvels of which our forefathers only dreamed, our railroads, our steamships, our motor transport system, and the planes that dot the sky are but the physical ingredients of our future success. They are as inanimate as a locomotive without power; they are dead things until the spirit of work is breathed into them by a working people.

Heavily armored door to one of the Treasury vaults is operated only by an armed guard, one of the uniformed forces of the U. S. Secret Service.

8

THE TEMPLES of Delphi and Delos in Greece were noted for the extensive banking activities that were carried on within their walls. In those early days it was more difficult to keep money than to earn it. Robbery, burglary, and banditry were so prevalent that those with large sums of money rarely went abroad without a bodyguard. There were few places where a man could keep his riches that were safe from marauders. That is why the massively built temples were used as safe deposit vaults in which money was placed under the protection of the State. Those authorized to receive the hoards of the panicky people saw an opportunity to turn what they considered an honest penny. They charged the depositors for the safekeeping of their hoarded earnings, and then loaned the money entrusted to them at interest rates ranging from ten to thirty per cent. Soon shrewd individuals, seeing the handsome profits to be made from handling other peoples' money, set up private banks. They built strong vaults, employed sturdy guards, and soon were doing a lively

FROM BENCH TO BANK

business. These private "bankers" were first heard of during the roaring days of Nebuchadnezzar about 600 B.C. They and their followers were a crafty lot, as may be gathered from the writings of Theocritus, Tacitus, and Suetonius.

The great bankers and money-lenders of the Middle Ages were Italian merchants who came principally from the cities of Lombardy and settled in London, Paris, and other large European centers. In London, the Lombardian money magnates segregated along a single thoroughfare later called Lombard Street. This became the financial center of London and attained world-wide prominence as a money mart.

Untrammeled by laws, and consumed with greed, these money-lenders built such an unsavory reputation that the name Lombard became a synonym for money-lender or usurer.

The Lombards, however, contributed much to the embryo business of banking. They learned their trade the hard way in the market place and on village streets. In their early days they were mostly itinerants who traveled from town to town and from door to door in pursuit of their money-lending activities. As some of them amassed riches, they settled in towns and large cities and set up a local banking business. They went to the open market place each morning, leading a bodyguard of several armed men who acted also as porters. Two carried a heavy oaken bench which the banker used as a counter and seat. It is from this bench that the modern bank gets its name. The Italian word *banco* means bench. Others of the men carried iron-bound money chests and leathern moneybags. The banker himself always carried the crude records that served as account books. When business was slack, he stood on his *banco* and exhorted the crowds to "step right up" and become independent at little cost.

Even in those early days, the loan shark was not unknown and while victims were not quite as plentiful as they are today, they fared quite as badly. The simple farmer who had spent in a wine shop the proceeds from his produce was an easy victim on whom to press a few florins. Months later after he had paid the banker many times the amount borrowed, he found himself still indebted for more than the original loan. As the itinerant banker migrated to other countries, he found a ready market for his usurious services and an unenviable reputation into the bargain.

At first the Italian banker's chief function was that of money changer. Practically every city issued its own coins, none of which were acceptable in a neighboring city. When a merchant of Florence came to Milan to make purchases, he visited first the banker or money-changer to convert his Florentine coins into Milanese equivalents. When his purchases were completed, he again visited the *banco* and changed what Milanese coins he had left into the coins of his own city, or, as sometimes happened, he found himself short of cash and was forced to borrow from his friend the *banco* man. Frequently, the merchant from out of town arrived destitute of even enough to buy a meal. Bandits had seen to it that he was cleaned out to the last coin. This was hard on merchant and banker alike, for the bankers did not consider a man who had had an encounter with the banditti a good credit risk for a loan.

The *banco* men from all over the country and adjoining territory got together and concocted a scheme to foil the bandits. Each of them placed in the keeping of the other a substantial sum of money, against which a customer could draw on presentation of a paper stating that he was entitled to a certain amount. The merchant from Florence could then journey to Milan without the responsibility of carrying a heavy load of silver and gold. In its place he carried a piece of paper for which the banker charged him a certain sum of money. It was worthless to the highwaymen, but as good as gold to the merchants. That piece of paper was nothing more than the bank draft as it is used today all over the world.

As the years passed, and bankers established themselves in the large cities throughout Europe, international trade assumed large proportions. Huge sums were involved in transactions between various countries. The merchant from Paris who made extensive purchases in Venice no longer had to send a heavy load of silver or gold coin in payment. A simple piece of paper did the job just as well, while the bandits, highwaymen, and robbers sat high above their native mountain roads, biting their nails and calling down maledictions on the bankers who had ruined their racket.

As communities became larger and local business increased, great quantities of coins changed hands daily. The purchaser drew from his store of money in the banker's keeping, and turned it over to the merchant from whom he bought a coat or a flask of wine. The merchant, at the end of the day, took the same money back to the banker for safekeeping overnight. This ebbing and flowing of money through the banker's hands gave him little chance to use it in loans, his most profitable activity. Then some shrewd person had a bright idea. If, he reasoned, a merchant can travel to several cities to make purchases without carrying so much as a florin with him, it should be possible to make purchases within his own city in the same manner. Soon a system was established whereby a person having money on deposit with a banker could, in lieu of coins, give the person from whom he purchased an article a piece of paper, on which he had written a note authorizing the banker to pay the bearer the amount of the purchase. In short, the check was invented. At first the people were chary of accepting these pieces of paper; in fact, none but those of known integrity could find much use for them. Bankers and businessmen alike favored the new money device and tried to encourage it in every way. It was not until the nineteenth century, however, that checks came into general use, and then only after stringent laws were established making the improper use of them a punishable offense.

Banking has come a long way since the banker straddled a bench in the market place. In the United States alone, there are some fifteen thousand banks in operation to say nothing of more than three thousand branches. To carry on the huge business of these banks, more than two hundred sixty-eight thousand people, of whom one-fifth are classed as officials, are employed. Formerly a *man's* business, banking now numbers among its employees some sixty thousand women, three thousand of whom hold executive positions.

The bank of today differs little in its functions from banks of long ago. It accepts money for safekeeping, and lends it at interest. It also sells drafts or bills of exchange so that its customers can make payments in other cities and countries without transporting the actual cash.

There are many variations of these basic activities, but they remain the essence of banking, whether the bank be large or small.

Broadly speaking, we have in the United States four types of banks that serve the public: national banks, state banks, trust companies, and savings banks. There is also the Federal Reserve System that operates twelve banks in important commercial centers. These are, however, bankers' banks with which the banking public has few dealings. All of these banks are rigidly regulated by the government, either state, or national, or both. Their charters are clear-cut declarations of what they may or may not do in their operations. Only in a few states are unchartered banks allowed to accept deposits or to perform certain other banking functions. A national bank receives its charter from the Comptroller of the Currency, who also is directly charged with its supervision. A state bank receives its charter from the legislature of the state in which it operates, or from some state government official or department empowered to issue bank charters.

A trust company is a corporation chartered and supervised by the state in which it operates and given authority to receive and execute trusts. A person of means may entrust his estate to a trust company, so that in the event of his death his debts are paid, his family is provided for, and his effects or their value are distributed according to his wishes in a legal and equitable manner. Many people desirous of having their future safeguarded against want or worry entrust their properties to trust companies which, in turn, skillfully manage the clients' affairs and judiciously invest their holdings. Many trust companies carry on an extensive banking business and many national banks are permitted by their charter to perform services similar to those of a trust company.

I had a neighbor, a professor in a large university, a man of exemplary character and with a fine intellectual background. He struggled for many years with the problem of making ends meet. His only extravagances were books and a small but complete workshop in the basement of his home. Besides his salary, he had a small income from

Currency packing room, Bureau of Engraving and Printing. Here sheets are counted, checked and packaged to await further operations.

a varied collection of securities left him by his father. His wife, a well-balanced and home-loving woman, did everything in her power to stretch the family funds to a point where they could put something aside for a rainy day.

One day, while returning to his home, the professor was struck by an automobile and severely injured. As the months dragged by it became evident that his speech was permanently impaired, that his career as a teacher was finished. Things looked black, indeed, until one day a lawyer called and informed him that a distant relative had died making him heir to a modest estate.

The lawyer, a kindly man with a broad knowledge of human nature, saw that the professor, intellectual though he was, lacked the ability to handle his affairs properly. During a later interview the attorney suggested that the newly acquired estate and the securities he owned be placed in the hands of a trust company. This was done without delay. Before many months the professor and his wife found themselves with an income slightly in excess of that which they had had before the accident, but it promised a secure future. With his affairs now handled skillfully by the trust company, and relieved of financial worry, the professor went to work in his basement shop on the development of several mechanical ideas he had been nursing for years. Within a few years he secured United States patents on three devices, one of which was bought on a royalty basis by a prominent manufacturer, all business arrangements being handled by the trust company. The professor who, as he often expressed it, was always "one jump ahead of the sheriff," was now on easy street.

The savings bank is intended primarily to provide those with modest means with a safe place to keep their money and receive reasonable returns from its safe investment. Many of the other banks, national, state, and trust companies, conduct savings departments where the savings of their clients are well-administered. These are not true savings institutions, however. They may not, for example, advertise for savings accounts in many states, and beyond a stipulated interest, they do not share their earnings with depositors.

The banks, organized for saving accounts exclusively, are called Mutual Savings Banks. They have no stockholders and no paid-in capital. Their earnings from the investments of their depositors' money are passed back to the depositors in proportion to their bal-

The result of inflation. A billion-mark note issued in Germany in January 1924. A hatful of these notes was necessary to buy a loaf of bread.

ances. Of course, some of the earnings are set aside to take care of the cost of doing business. These mutual savings banks are hedged around with every safety precaution. They may, for instance, place the depositors' money only in certain approved types of investment. They do not accept checking accounts, and discourage the promiscuous withdrawal of funds. Their job is to encourage savings among the great mass of the people so as to build a country-wide fund for the rainy day. This national nest-egg is huge for in the mutual savings banks of the United States are stored nearly twelve billion dollars.

Prior to December, 1913, the banks of the United States were in the position of the shoemaker who did a fine job on his customers shoes while his own remained in poor condition. American banks gave excellent service to their customers, supplying every facility and convenience physical and financial. In spite of their best efforts, however, the financial status of the country was periodically subjected to violent ups and downs. Panic was a specter always peering around the corner, frightening the most substantial of bankers out of their wits. The preponderance of depositors' funds was merely loans to the bank which could be called for at any time. Under normal conditions, a large share of the bank deposits could be loaned out safely and with profitable returns provided, of course, there was enough money, or its equivalent, kept in reserve to take care of ordinary emergencies. It sometimes happened that when these emergencies arose, they quickly developed into crises that soon became nation-wide. A frequent phenomenon of these crises was a "run on the bank," a wide-spread stampede of emotionally unbalanced people bent on withdrawing their deposits, and thereby bringing about the very thing they feared—the closing of the bank. Often it happened that banks normally solvent were unable to meet the simultaneous demands of the depositors, with the result that they had to close their doors.

In those days prior to 1913 the banks, refuge of depositors when money was scarce, had no refuge to which to turn in a crisis. In other words, the depositor who found himself in a tight place could rush to his bank and borrow a thousand dollars to tide him over, while the bank with depleted reserve had no place to turn for the million or half-million dollars it needed in its crisis.

In December, 1913, the Federal Reserve System was organized. It embodied among other features twelve super banks known as Federal Reserve banks and located in as many commercially important cities. As customers, these super banks had about five thousand national banks and about one thousand one hundred state banks. In the case of the national banks, membership in the System was obligatory, while the state banks were admitted to membership only after they had qualified as eligible.

The Federal Reserve banks function for their banker customers in practically the same manner as the local banks serve their depositors. That is to say, each bank must carry a certain amount of its reserves on deposit with its Federal Reserve bank. It may draw against this deposit reserve, or increase it by borrowing under the supervision of the Federal Reserve.

The capital of the Federal Reserve banks, which are non-profit-making, comes entirely from the number of banks listed as members which receive dividends that may not exceed six per cent.

The financial panic of 1933, during which all banks were closed as a safety precaution, proved again the necessity of protecting the small depositor against the inexplicable whims of money in the mass.

During that chaotic period, hundreds of banks that were basically

During the French Revolution, the landed property of the clergy was confiscated by the Assembly. To raise ready money, bonds known as "assignats" were issued on the security of the land. Since these bonds represented land assigned to the holder, they were used as money. One of the greatest fiascos in history followed. The "assignats" carried the line, "The law will punish counterfeiters with death. Informers will be rewarded by the nation."

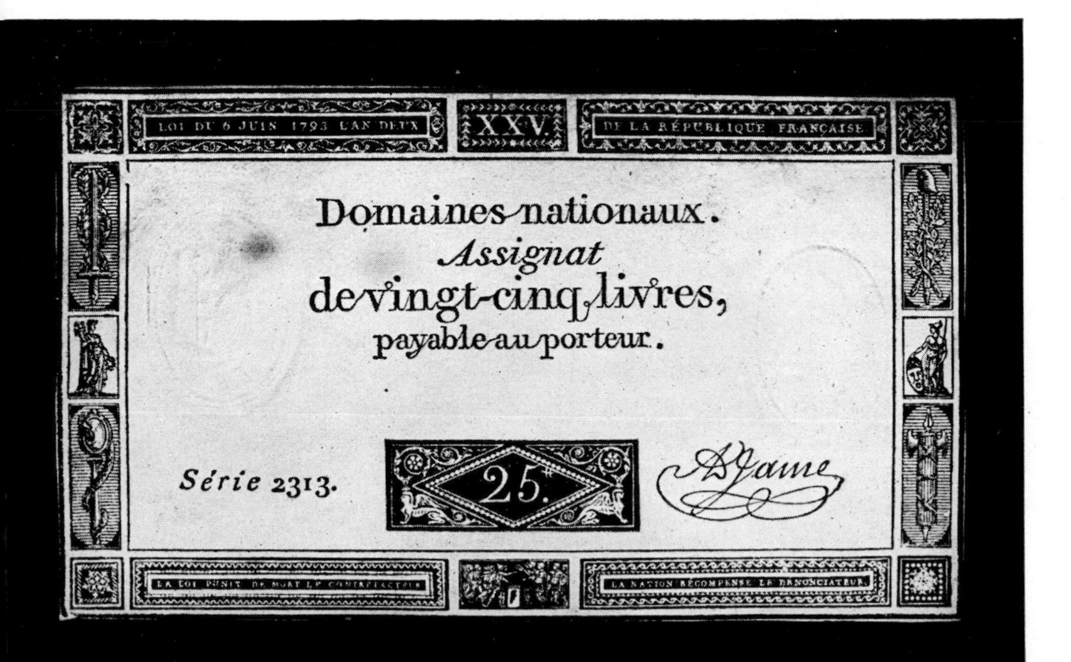

sound found themselves caught in the path of the financial hurricane that strewed the country with bank wreckage. The public, knowing little of the bankers' problems and caring less, blamed them for the catastrophe their own mass fear had brought about. On one of those unforgettable days when banks were crashing by scores daily, I saw a line of people two blocks in length waiting for a bank to open its doors. Terror was in every face, the same mute fear I had seen on the faces of passengers after a steamer collision. For the most part they were silent, morose. A few were belligerent; all were emotionally unbalanced. The people in line were a cross section of the community. Men with dinner pails rubbed elbows with local merchants. Women wearing shawls crowded forward against women in rich furs. Boys and girls were sandwiched between grandfathers and grandmothers. A lawyer in the line was besieged with questions as to the legality of the whole thing. A doctor was called out of line to attend a hysterical woman. "Hold my place!" he said to the man next to him as he went to his duty.

Within the bank, in plain sight, were bills and silver stacked cage-high. Tellers, affable as usual, worked like beavers, paying and paying. As depositors were satisfied, their brief look of relief gave way to embarrassment and then to shame as they slunk away. One man paused at the teller's window. "Never mind," he said as he passed back the bundle of bills he had received. He went out with his head high.

The futility, as well as the danger of depositors, swarming down on a bank and demanding their deposits may be gathered from the fact that the total amount of cash in the United States is but a fraction of the combined deposits. This condition is not only approved by the law of the land, but is endorsed by the laws of economics.

This phenomenon of mass fear is as old as human emotions, and as unpredictable. It is as uncontrollable as a stampeding herd, but is preventable by removing its cause.

It was with the purpose of eliminating this mass fear that the Federal Deposit Insurance Corporation was formed after the panic of 1933. Its charter provides that each depositor of member banks is insured against loss to the amount of five thousand dollars, if the bank should close for any reason. More than thirteen thousand national and state banks with deposits of about fifty-four billion dollars have been freed from the fear of a "run" by membership in the corporation.

Through this co-operation between government and banking, the great mass of people whose deposits rarely exceed five thousand dollars can feel secure even in times of financial stress.

One of the most astonishing phases of the business of banking is the system by which the billions of checks used annually in carrying on the nation's business are credited or debited to the banks. This operation is carried out in a "clearing house."

The banks in towns, cities, states, and the country at large are organized in groups known as Clearinghouse Associations. There is also an international Clearinghouse.

The procedure of a clearinghouse, particularly a large one, is both complicated and confusing to the lay person, yet so perfectly ordered is each step of its work, it ends each day during which it shuffles millions of dollars in the form of checks without a penny left over or a penny short. Each bank receives the money due it, or pays that which it owes. All this is done with a trifling transfer of actual cash. The accounts between all the banks in the United States are settled daily with a cash transfer of less than five per cent of the total payments.

A simplification of the clearing house process is something like this:

In a small town there are two banks, A and B. During a day's business, A receives 100 checks drawn on B for a total of $1,000. On the same day B receives 120 checks drawn on A for a total of $1,050. The following morning a representative of bank A meets a representative of bank B. On comparing the totals of each bank's batch of checks, it is found that B owes A $50 for which he promptly gives A a check, and that is all there is to it. Although $2,050 are involved in the transaction, only $50 change hands.

In actual practice of course, A would have checks from many banks other than B. The procedure would be the same, however.

Like manufacturers, wholesalers or retailers, banks are in business for profit. According to the figures of the Federal Deposit Insurance

Portrait from a counterfeit one-dollar bill.

Corporation, which covers ninety-seven per cent of all commercial banks in the United States, nearly half a bank's profits come from loans, and one-third comes from interest on securities.

Loans, therefore, may be likened to the steel skeleton around which the bank structure is built. If the steel is strong and well-engineered, the building will stand the shock of the hurricane and the ravages of time. That accounts for the extreme caution with which the banker makes his loans.

Quite recently, I saw a shopkeeper in a small town plead with his banker for an unsecured loan. He needed the money for merchandise he was about to purchase. The banker gently, but firmly, refused. A week later I passed the merchant's store which was but a

Portrait from a genuine one-dollar bill.

block away from the bank building. The door was closed and on it was pinned a note which read: "Gone fishing. Back tomorrow." The banker knew his man.

Since much of the bank's income is earned from successful loans, the banker is just as anxious to sell his wares as is the grocer or the butcher. If he is hesitant or refuses, it is usually because he considers the applicant for the loan a poor risk. Handling other people's money, he is more cautious than he probably would be in handling his own funds. It is this meticulous care, coupled with skill and knowledge that has enabled the banker to *create* most of the money with which the country does its business.

In all, there are only about seventeen billion dollars in coin and paper currency in the United States, yet bank deposits are nearly eight times that amount or one hundred twenty billion dollars. That may sound contradictory, yet it is perfectly logical. Let us assume that a large bank buys half a million dollars' worth of United States Treasury bonds; this is what happens: The Treasurer of the United States has an account in the bank, just like any other depositor. The bank credits this account with half a million dollars and receives from the Treasury half a million dollars' worth of bonds. It now has the bonds and the money, thus doubling its reserves. Later the Treasurer will draw on his account in the bank to pay certain government obligations. Some of these drafts will, in all likelihood, go to depositors of the bank for goods or services. These customers deposit the drafts, thus increasing their balances as the Treasury balance is reduced. Let us suppose that one of these depositors is a manufacturer who employs a large number of people in the community. He draws against his balance for his pay roll, thus reducing it. However, many of his employees will also be depositors in the bank and will increase their deposits with the checks received from their employer. In turn, the employees draw against their deposits to pay the butcher and the baker. Some of these checks will also make their way back to the bank since the merchants are also depositors.

Now, if we consider all the banks as a group, we find that their balances have increased as a direct result of the purchase of that half-million dollars' worth of bonds. That is how the bank creates money not only for itself, but for other banks as well, and adds to the financial strength of the country.

One of the most commendable services of modern banking is the encouragement of small borrowers to come to their bank for the modest sums they require in an emergency. This has saved thousands from the clutches of loan sharks and usurers. Large cities and industrial areas are often infested with these ravenous creatures who prey on the unwary and through fear, and often force, keep them in virtual slavery sometimes for years.

In a certain plant in an eastern city a young mechanic of excellent character found himself confronted by a grave financial problem. Illness and death had come to his family, leaving him heavily in debt. One day during lunch hour he confided his troubles to a man who worked at the next bench. "Aw, forget it!" said the other. "I know a guy who'll fix you up. You can pay it back a little at a time, but be sure you don't mention it to anyone around the plant."

The next day the two men went to a sandwich shop for lunch. A well-dressed man of middle age was waiting near the door. The young mechanic was introduced to him. The stranger was affable and sympathetic. "How much do you need?" he asked.

"A hundred dollars would help out a lot," the young man replied.

"Okay," said the stranger, pulling out a roll of bills from which he peeled a hundred dollars. "Here you are, kid," he said cheerfully, "your worries are over. Here, sign this!" He pushed a paper in front of the young mechanic and handed him a fountain pen. The young man signed it. Dazed at his good fortune, he didn't even read it. "That will set you back only twelve dollars a week," the loan shark said casually as they parted.

As the weeks passed the victim made his payments promptly to a collector who hung around the entrance to the plant. On the ninth week, having paid $108, the mechanic said cheerfully to the collector, "That about cleans it up, doesn't it?" The collector turned on him savagely, "What do you mean, clean it up?" he snarled. "You ain't started to pay it off yet. You been paying the interest. Better make it twenty bucks next week or else!"

For a moment the machinist was stunned; then he realized he had been trapped. "Okay," he said sullenly and left. The following morning when he reached his bench, he found that his fellow-worker who had introduced him to the loan shark had disappeared. He also learned that two employees had been waylaid and beaten. Casting aside his fears, he went to the plant superintendent and told his story. The boss, a direct man, stormed for a moment. "Serves you fellows right for being such suckers!" he exploded. Then more gently he said, "Don't worry! We've already taken action against those men." That evening the loan shark and several of his "contact men" were arrested, and among them was the employee who had introduced the victim to the suave and sympathetic stranger who proved to be the head of a ruthless band of money gorillas.

Not all the victims of lawless money lenders are as fortunate

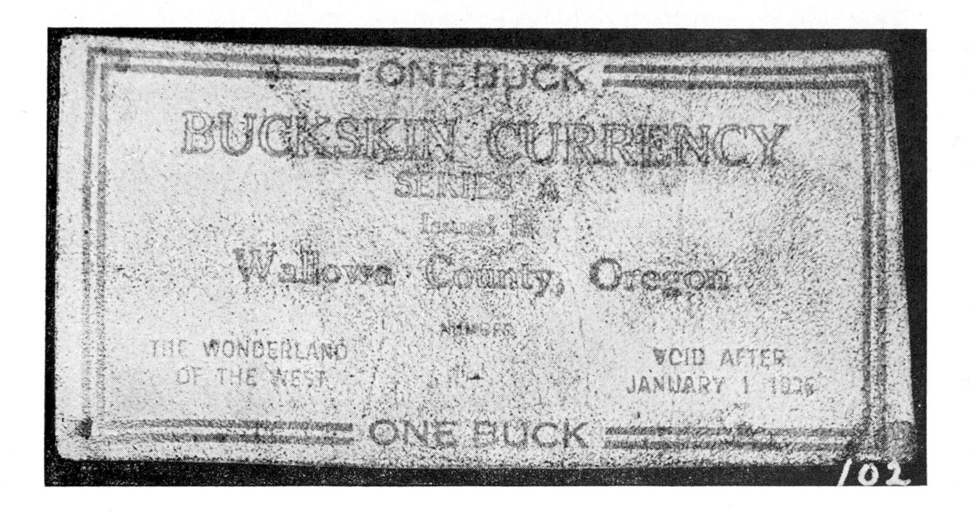

A leather dollar issued by Wallowa County, Oregon, during the 1933 crisis.

as was the young mechanic. Many of them are kept in subjection for long periods during which they are mulcted of many times the trifling amount of the loan through threats and violence.

Another type of money lender, while operating within the law, is quite as ruthless as his gorilla brother. He makes his loans only when there is valuable collateral—an automobile, household goods, or real estate. He operates on a basis of repayment of the loan with interest in weekly or monthly installments. As long as payments are kept up to the minute, relations with these money lenders are pleasant enough, but if for any reason the borrower is unable to meet an installment, he finds his property seized and a costly fight on his hands to get it back.

A young man I know borrowed two hundred dollars from one of these finance "services," putting up his automobile as collateral. The loan interest and service charges were to be paid in six equal monthly installments. He made five payments promptly. Two days before the final payment was due, the firm by which he was employed sent him on business to several cities. The trip took longer than he expected; he did not return for a week. On arrival at his home his wife told him excitedly that the car had been stolen from the garage that evening. He notified the local police at once. The police soon informed him that the car had been seized by the finance company. Next morning he hurried to the finance company's office with a check in his pocket for the final payment. The manager was very regretful, but business was business. The car had been turned over to another company. It took days of time and endless trouble for the borrower to recover his car. Before he could get it back, however, he had to pay $137, supposedly spent in fees and incomprehensible expenses. At no time did the finance company step outside the law.

If a reputable bank refuses a loan, the would-be borrower should consider himself lucky rather than unlucky, since it means in plain language that the banker, expert in finance and in judging human nature, does not believe that the applicant can repay the loan. It is equivalent to advising him that a loan from any source will increase rather than ease his financial worries.

GOOD MONEY LOOKS GOOD.

BECAUSE
It is made by experts.

BECAUSE
It is made on costly machines designed just for that purpose.

BECAUSE
It is printed from steel plates produced by the best engravers.

BECAUSE
It IS good.

9

ONE EVENING not so long ago, I spent several hours in the crew's quarters aboard an ocean-going vessel. A driving rain sluiced along the decks, and sheets of freezing spray battered the superstructure. It was cozy in the smoke-filled recreation room where half-a-dozen bronzed men whiled away the hours of their watch below. Sailors of all nationalities will argue among themselves on the slightest provocation and on any subject. As a class, I have found them better informed than most groups whose days are spent in heavy work. This is, perhaps, because of their frequent contact with the customs and manners of other peoples and their constant readiness to converse with whomever they chance to meet. Or it may be because, more than other workers, they are brought closer to the irresistible forces of nature. No one, no matter how small his mentality, can stand on the deck of a ten-thousand-ton ship when she is being buffeted around like a chip in a mill-race without giving thought to how pitifully puny man and his mightiest works really are. During many

I ASKED THE MAN WHO KNEW

a storm, while death stalked beside the ship, I have seen the salt-crusted faces of sailors express reverence in every feature for the unseen wind against which they were battling and for the towering combers that charged snarling down on them. I have observed the thoughtful silence that grips them for days after one of their number has been snatched away by the sea. The sea makes one *think.*

Two of the men in the crew's quarters had been fishermen, sailing out of Gloucester, Massachusetts for a dozen years before shipping on deep-water vessels. Two had sailed the Great Lakes for half-a-dozen summers, and worked in a certain automobile plant in Detroit during the winter months when ice closes the Lakes to navigation. Barney, the eldest of the group and a grizzled old salt, left home when he was fourteen and had completed his forty-third year at sea. The youngest of the group was a lad of nineteen named Nils. Nils had been a shipping clerk in a Minneapolis flour mill.

The Lake sailors were high school graduates; Nils left high school during his junior year. The Gloucester men had finished the primary grades and had left school to earn a living. Barney boasted only a number of degrees from the school of hard knocks, but he could hold his own, or better, with the younger men. On that particular evening the argument waxed strong. The point at issue was whether the same opportunities for a young man to become financially successful exist today as they did a quarter of a century ago.

Old Barney insisted that modern business, hungry for profits, gave little chance to the young man to rise from the ranks, and that the unions had so regimented men and wages that personal initiative counted for little. One of the fresh-water sailors took issue, pointing out there was more room at the top today than ever before. The older of the Gloucester men broke in belligerently:

"Here I am with nine years at sea!" he shouted, "and I am no better off today than when I started."

"And whose fault is that?" queried the man from the Lakes.

The New Englander paused a moment while his wrath mounted. The unwritten law of the sea forbade loud voices while men were asleep near by. "It's the fault of sculpins like you, always siding with the bosses!" he growled.

The young man stood up, leaning gracefully against the roll of the ship and approached his antagonist. "Listen, you poor swab," he said quietly, "I'll tell you whose fault it is. You've been at sea for nine years, and you're still as dumb about seamanship as you were the first time you stepped on a deck. You can't turn in a decent splice. You can't use the palm-and-needle. You can sling a paint-brush, but you know nothing about paint or what it is made of. You've put in as many tricks at the wheel as the next man, but you know nothing about navigation, and care less. Sure, you're strong and willing, we all know that. You can put your beef on a line or bend an oar double—so what! You work eight hours a day and you sleep eight. What do you do with the remaining eight? I'll tell you. You kill time instead of using it on something that will give you a boost someday. Maybe you're waiting for the skipper, or the mate, or the bosun to come along and take you by the hand and make a better sailor of you!"

The young man's sarcasm bit deep. There was silence for a moment. Old Barney who had joined in many a fo'c'stle battle of words, removed his pipe and rasped:

"I've heard sea lawyers like you before. But where does it get you? How much better off are *you* than the rest of us?"

The Lake sailor hesitated.

"Yeah!" chorused the men. "What does all that baloney get you?"

"We don't see any gold braid on you!" chimed in the Gloucester man.

"Just a minute," said the young man, reaching into his hip pocket. He bashfully drew out his wallet and took from it a green paper.

"This is what it got me," he said quietly. "While we were in port I sat for an exam as third mate. Here's my ticket."

Seafaring men may argue to the point of violence, but they are quick to acknowledge defeat.

"Okay, sailor! You win!" said one of the men.

"Glad you made it," said another.

One by one the sailors took their oil-skins from their lockers and went on deck. The eight to twelve watch was about to begin.

That evening I sat late with the captain while we discussed many things, including men and their work. I told him of the episode in the crew's quarters and of the sailor with the third mate's ticket.

"I know all about him," he said. "He is a good man and he knows his business. I would not be surprised if he shipped out as third mate on one of our new ships after this voyage."

Weeks later, while in Detroit, I spent some time with the president of the automobile company for which the Lake sailor had worked. He was a young man, as top-flight executives go, slender, alert, and with eyes keen as needle points. His office, unlike those of many executives I had visited, was austere as a monk's cell. It was a workshop, an integral part of the great factory, the G. H. Q. of an army of some fifteen thousand men and women contributing their strength and their skill to building America through motor transportation.

As we walked through the miles of aisles in the huge plant, and watched the miracle of an automobile assembly line, I soon observed that the president was personally familiar with every operation and every part, be it ever so small, and every tool for the entire length of the line. He was at home in the dust-filled foundry or among the thundering trip-hammers that fashioned white hot billets into intricate parts.

That evening after dinner with the president and his family, I discovered the secret of his familiarity with the tools and appliances of the industry. Seated in his well-stocked library, among furnishings as American as one might find in Old Salem, I learned that the industrial leader with whom I was chatting had started his career in a humble garage as a mechanic's helper. He had neither pull nor influence, save that created by the whole-heartedness he put into his work and his unending effort to prepare himself for the next job above him. More than once, while we conversed, I thought of the young sailor and his first step upward.

As the evening passed, our conversation converged toward the opportunities and responsibilities of youth in the rehabilitation of the world. And it was then I learned some of the simple philosophies of a man who had started at the bottom and worked his way to the pinnacle of his industry.

"Let us take the subject of money," he said, "and let us assume that a lad works faithfully and intelligently, and is paid accordingly. He will not attain complete success unless he puts as much intelligence and effort into the management of that money as he put into earning it. Wealth, whether it is of a nation or an individual, can be increased only through the thrift and frugal management that will produce eventually what we call 'savings.' It is the savings of individuals, partnerships, and corporations that make possible the birth of industries and the increase of facilities and working capital for growth and expansion."

"Is it not true," I asked, "that much of our American business is done on a credit basis?"

"Yes," he replied. "Credit can be a good substitute for money if the borrower is worthy of the trust placed in him by the lender. Few people have a full understanding of the pledge they make when seeking credit. It means in substance: 'In return for this loan I promise to work harder or longer hours, and if necessary deny myself some of the things to which I have been accustomed, in order to pay you back.' In other words the borrower says, 'I will produce more and consume less, so that there will be enough of my income left over to pay the loan.' "

"Anything that money can purchase," he went on, "represents only labor, physical or mental. The man with a thousand or a million dollars derives no income from his money, unless he sets it to work by loaning it for the purchase of labor or investing it in an enterprise that will employ labor. Banks can pay interest only be-

Heavily armored truck used by the U. S. Treasury for transport of money.

Alcatraz, the Federal prison, where counterfeiters spend years regretting they matched wits with the U. S. Secret Service.

cause they put their depositors' money to work in manufacturing, commercial, and other enterprises that require labor to carry on. It is the result of this labor that makes the profits from which the bank loan is paid. And from the money made on the loan by the bank, the depositor gets his share in the form of interest."

The simple directness with which this man of big business spoke interested me. Not once did he dwell upon the huge problems that confronted him daily in directing the affairs of a large corporation, to say nothing of the financial and physical welfare of an army of workers.

"Do those simple principles apply to a corporation, as they do to an individual?" I asked.

"Yes," he said thoughtfully. "Broadly speaking, they apply to all who receive and spend money. If more is spent than is received, trouble is just around the corner—and that goes for the million-dollar corporation or for the twenty-dollar-a-week clerk." He paused for a moment.

"Speaking of corporations," he continued, "it is surprising how many people think that the executive officers of a large corporation own the business, when the fact is that the average large corporation is owned by thousands of people. I know of one that has more than three hundred thousand owners. These owners are the stockholders to whom all the officers are responsible, just as is any other employee. The president can be 'fired' just as quickly as the office boy. A vice-president holds his job on the same basis as a file clerk. Both are measured by the yardstick of industry and loyalty.

"The large enterprises we have in America would not exist today, were it not for the millions of stockholders who invested their savings in them. There are few individuals who could personally finance such large undertakings alone. Some of our great manufacturing corporations have stated that for every worker in their employ, they have invested eight to twelve thousand dollars in specialized machinery that will turn out goods in great volume at low prices. In some of these plants the cost of mechanical equipment alone runs into many millions of dollars."

"What advice would you give to young people who are anxious to become successful?" I asked.

My host paused a moment as his thoughts flew back to his own

Pouring "melt" from electric furnace at the Philadelphia Mint.

early working days. "Live according to a budget," he said. "Nearly everyone knows approximately what his monthly income is. Therefore, it is easy to budget. Take pencil and paper and set down first the month's income. Then list such fixed expenses as rent, food, monthly payments on debts; in fact, all expenses that must be met monthly, not forgetting a certain percentage of the income to be set aside for savings. When those fixed charges are added up and subtracted from the income, the remainder is what can be spent for entertainment and other non-essentials."

Then with characteristic candor he added:

"Many of us spend first and worry afterward. We hope that in some way we can stretch our income to cover our bills. But that hope is seldom realized."

The chiming of a clock warned me that it was time for me to leave. My host drove me to the Detroit Athletic Club where I was stopping. His car was one of the millions his factory had turned out, and was by no means of the latest vintage.

"I see you drive one of your own make," I ventured.

"Why not?" he replied. "There is no better car."

I agreed with him for I had driven one of them for several years. "You have much to be proud of," I said.

After a pause he replied modestly:

"Not so much when we remember that man has never created any material thing in all the span of his existence. He has merely moved materials from one place to another, and changed their form or built them according to a prescribed plan. Therefore, when we consider the cost of a locomotive, a house, or an automobile, we are dealing with units of labor that man has applied to God-given materials. It is this labor, whether it is physical or mental, that determines our monetary wealth."

After I had stepped from the car and bade my host "Good night," he repeated as he shifted gears:

"Remember that money is merely a token of labor performed."